GOLF
Play Like A Pro

Sports Illustrated Winner's Circle Books

BOOKS ON TEAM SPORTS

Baseball
Football: Winning Defense
Football: Winning Offense
Hockey
Lacrosse
Pitching

BOOKS ON INDIVIDUAL SPORTS

Bowling
Competitive Swimming
Golf
Racquetball
Skiing
Tennis
Track: Championship Running

SPECIAL BOOKS

Canoeing
Fly Fishing
Scuba Diving
Strength Training

Sports Illustrated
GOLF
Play Like A Pro

by Mark Mulvoy

Photography by
Heinz Kluetmeier

Sports Illustrated
Winner's Circle Books
New York

Photo credits: Mickey Pfleger, p. 8; Manny Millan, p. 54 (bottom); Bill Jaspersohn, pp. 10, 18, 19, 20, 21, 22, 24, 28, 40, 43, 95; courtesy of The Old Golf Shop, Cincinnati, Ohio, p. 14, illustration, p. 17; courtesy of the Acushnet Company, Titleist Golf Division, pp. 22, 45 (bottom); Mitch Pizzetti, courtesy of Lynx Golf Equipment, pp, 34, 35; John D. Hanlon, pp, 64, 74, 92; James Drake, p. 78; Tony Tomsic, pp, 88, 89; Jacqueline Duvoisin, pp. 12, 64; John Iacono, pp. 17, 92, 120; Steve Powell, p. 50; Neil Leifer, p. 78; Andy Hayt, p. 121; Walter Iooss, Jr., p. 148; all other photographs by Heinz Kluetmeier.

Library of Congress Cataloging-in-Publication Data

Mulvoy, Mark.
  Sports illustrated golf.

  1. Golf. I. Kluetmeier, Heinz. II. Title
GV965.M75 1988 796.352   87-32381
ISBN 0-452-26098-1 (pbk.)   88 89 90 91 92 AG/HL 10 9 8 7 6 5 4 3 2 1

Contents

Sports Illustrated
GOLF
Play Like A Pro

Introduction

Most touring professional golfers worth a week's supply of free golf balls are forever talking about the so-called "secrets" of the golf swing or about special golf clubs or balls or grips or even prayers that can turn the most innocent newcomer to the game into the next U.S. Open champion. But the real "secret" to golf—the only secret—is the development of a fundamentally sound swing pattern, one that will not self-destruct on, say, the eighteenth tee when you have a 1-up lead on your opponent in the finals of the Class C club championship. This swing pattern must be built not on secrets, not on gimmicks, but on solid principles. It must be built not in front of the bedroom mirror, not in the back yard, but on the practice tee.

No one has ever said that golf is an easy game to play. It is, however, probably easier than you have been making it. The trick is to maintain your cool, to relax on the course. And how do you accomplish this? By having one golf swing that works, not a dozen swings that never work.

Yes, keep it simple and keep it cool. Most people worry too much about their games and their swings. There is no reason to fidget over every shot as though the U.S. Open championship were at stake. Wind direction . . . downhill

A sound swing is the key to a successful golf game.

lie . . . trap in front . . . have I got the right club . . . maybe a six-iron would be better . . . spread the feet a little wider . . . play the ball back . . . where are the Vs pointing . . . is my shirt tucked in . . . ?

Relax. Accept the fact that not all your shots will be perfect. Even the best players mis-hit the golf ball a few times each round. When you leave the clubhouse and head for the first tee, face the fact that you are going to hit a certain number of bad shots. It's the only way to survive on the course. How many times have you played golf with someone who missed a shot, got mad, and for that reason mis-hit the next shot too? There is nothing sillier than having a temper tantrum on the golf course just because you didn't hit the perfect shot.

The fact can easily be forgotten in the heat of play, but in golf, fun is the name of the game.

In playing golf, the only swing you should ever worry about is your own. And remember, there really is no such thing as a perfect golf swing. Some are better than others, but even the best have flaws. When Jack Nicklaus was at his peak, many so-called doctors of the golf swing argued that he had a major flaw in his swing because his right elbow rode out on the backswing. Maybe it did, but it never bothered Nicklaus on his trips to the bank. These swing doctors tend to find alleged flaws in all swings. They say Lanny Wadkins has a swing that's too fast and too wristy, and complain that Tom Watson's is too mechanical. Arnold Palmer doesn't swing at the ball, they say; he swipes at it. Tell that to his accountant. One of the best pure swings on the Tour belongs to Curtis Strange, twice the leading-money winner in the 1980s. His swing is

Patty Sheehan: perfect form for power.

long and rhythmic, the picture of style and grace. But at impact, Strange is in essentially the same position as Nicklaus, Palmer, Watson—and, for that matter, all the young hotshots burning up the Tour these days. They just get to the impact point in different ways.

All golfers tend to fall into one of two categories: They are either "hitters" or "swingers." A hitter usually takes a fast, abrupt, muscular, complicated swipe at the ball. That's fine, if you are six feet five, weigh 250 pounds, and used to be Mr. America. Hitters must play golf almost every day in order to maintain mechanical coordination during their swing. The men's pro golf tour is a haven for hitters—players who hit hundreds and hundreds of golf balls each and every day of the week.

Do you play golf every day? Probably not. You have to work for a living. In fact, if you play golf even twice in seven days, you've had a big week. So how can you expect to be a hitter and attack a golf ball? You can't. What you must do is become a swinger. Only swingers can expect to play the game of golf once or twice a week with consistently good results.

Look at it this way. You swing a club anywhere from thirty-five to seventy-five times a round, not counting putts. Since you probably play infrequently, you can hardly expect to keep a fast, jerky, muscular, complicated swing pattern in a working groove that many times in a round. Sure, you might hit a few good shots in succession, but soon your timing will fall apart—and with that the rest of your game will probably collapse too.

The object, then, is to find one sound swing that works for you—and keep making it work. This book will detail for you the mechanics of the golf swing that will work more consistently all day, every day—one that will keep the ball in play. A swing that will not get you into trouble. A swing that you will be able to trust. A swing that will not prompt you to smash your five-iron against a tree or throw your pitching wedge into a lagoon. A swing that requires very little physical strain and is easy to repeat throughout your round. A swing based on solid fundamentals. A swing made for you. A swing made for everyone. But this swing will work only if you work at making it work. On the practice tee.

For all you lefties out there, remember that everything discussed in subsequent chapters holds true for you as well, except that specific instructions should be "mirrored"; that is, when the left shoulder is mentioned, think right shoulder, right knee, think left, and so on.

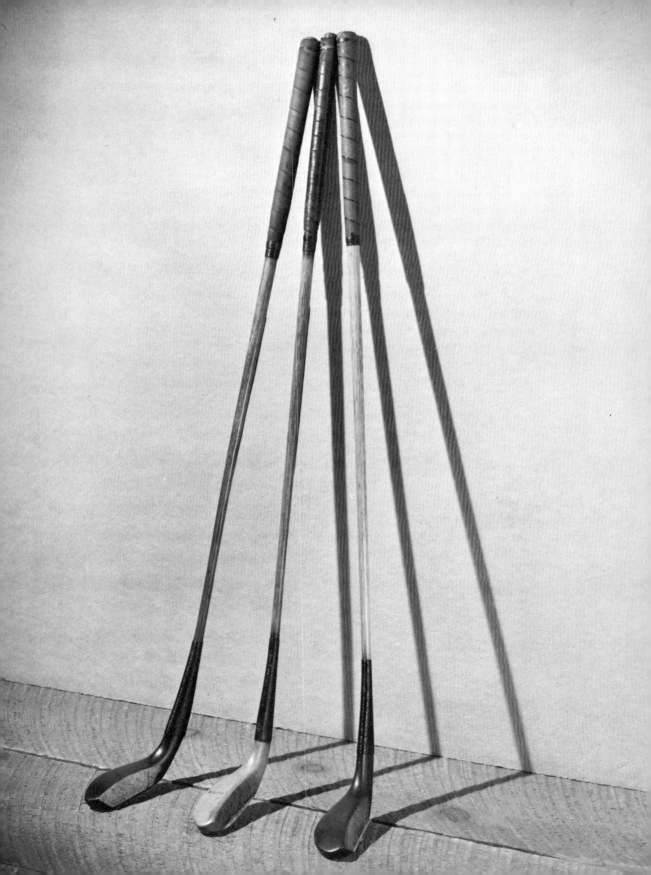

1

The Game

With apologies to the Dutch, the Italians, the Germans, and various other people who stubbornly maintain that they invented the game of golf, this sport that has tortured so many and rewarded so few was first played not in Rome, not along the Rhone, but in Scotland, way back in the fifteenth century. Historians generally agree that the word *golf* comes from a Germanic word *Kolbe,* which means "club." But the grand old game in which the competitors used a *Kolbe* was more like shinny, or hockey, than anything else. Indeed, there is no question that it was the Scots who first took club in hand, flailed away at some type of ball or rock, and attempted to deposit said object into a hole in the ground, without encountering opposition from a rival. Unfortunately, there is no record of who made the first hole-in-one or, for that matter, the first triple bogey.

There are 18 *holes* in a standard round of golf, all of which must be played in proper order. If you skip from, say, the fourth green to the eleventh tee, then from the eleventh green to the fifth tee, you cannot post an official score for your 18-hole round. Generally, a hole consists of everything from the tee to the green. Specifically, the hole is a cup 4¼ inches in diameter that is

15

A set of fine old woods circa 1870. Note the curved beech heads and hickory shafts.

sunk a minimum of 4 inches below the putting surface. The object of golf is to get the ball from the tee and into the hole in the least number of shots.

Officially, a hole begins at the teeing ground, or as most people call it, the *tee*. The golf ball is set upon a wooden peg, also called a tee. On each teeing ground there are usually at least three sets of markers, which can vary from large balls, to driftwood, to rocks, to statues, etc. These markers indicate the teeing-off spot for a hole, and they're set in such a way that you can play the same golf course at varying lengths. As a general rule, the markers are called red, white and blue. The red markers define the so-called ladies' course and are placed on that part of the tee that is closest to the green. The white markers are set between the red markers and the blue markers; they define the mid-length course that the great majority of golfers prefer to play. The blue markers define the championship course, "championship" meaning that the course is stretched to its maximum yardage. As a rule only professionals and the better amateurs play the blue markers.

As the ball is set upon the tee, it must not be ahead of the markers; in fact, the ball must be between the markers and, at the same time, not more than two club lengths behind them. While the ball must be within these confines, the player may position himself outside the area. Once you strike your tee shot, the hole is underway.

Honor is a word you will hear frequently on the course, as in, "Who's got the honor?" In golf, honor means the privilege of playing first off the tee, and the honor always belongs to the player who completed the previous hole in the fewest strokes.

En route from the tee to the green, you will encounter either the fairway or the rough, if not both, and may well find hazards in both. The fairway is the short grass, as the pros call it; to put it another way, the fairway is what you'd like your lawn to look like. The rough is a variety of things: long grass, rocks, trees, bushes, pathways, etc. Hazards come in two forms: bunkers and water. When you hear the word *bunker,* think of sand, as in sand traps. When you think of water, imagine lakes, creeks, ponds, lagoons, oceans, rivers, gulfs, and ditches. You can step into a bunker and attempt to extricate your ball with the swing of a club. However, when you hit the ball into a water hazard, you invariably will be forced to take a one-stroke penalty and drop your ball somewhere along the line that your original shot took to its watery grave.

You should check the official rules of golf to gain a better understanding of the various penalties and the drop procedures, but whenever you are hitting from the area of a hazard, remember that it is against the rules to ground your club in that hazard. Penalty: one stroke.

The changing faces of golf course architecture: the old (top), created by God; the new (bottom), created by man.

Golfers usually refer to the groomed longer grass fringing the fairways (left) as the "rough," while the "deep rough" is any ungroomed portion of the course (center). Water hazards are often defined by stakes. In most cases, when a golfer loses a ball in a water hazard, he's required by the

All golf holes have a predetermined par, *par* being the number of strokes a first-rate golfer is expected to need to get his ball from the tee to the cup. Golf holes come in three pars: par threes, par fours, and par fives. Generally, a par three is any hole up to 260 yards long; a par four hole is one between 260 yards and 475 yards; and a par five hole is one longer than 475 yards. Most golf courses have a total 18-hole par of 72, with the holes consisting of 10 par fours, four par fives and four par threes. In terms of putting, par is always two strokes per hole. So, on a par three, for instance, a "routine" par means hitting your tee shot onto the green and then taking two putts for your three.

A *birdie* is a score that is one stroke less than par; an *eagle* is a score that is two strokes fewer than par; a *double eagle,* the rarest of birds, is a score that is three strokes fewer than par. On the other side, a *bogey* is a score that is one

rules of golf to position himself nearest the ball's point of entry and a maximum of two club lengths from the stake. Then, looking at the hole, he drops a new ball at arm's length in front of him. Penalty for the drop: one shot.

shot more than par, a *double bogey* is two over par, a *triple bogey* three over, etc.

Essentially, golf is played in two ways: match or stroke. In match play, the most common form of play among amateurs, the game is played by holes —one player against the other, one side against the other, lowest score winning each hole. In stroke play, the usual form of competition among professionals, the golfer who completes his or her round, or tournament, in the least number of strokes is the victor.

One of the first "in" terms you will hear on a golf course is *Nassau,* but don't call your travel agent. Put simply, Nassau is the term for the match-play competition preferred by most amateurs, and also by professionals when they are playing practice rounds against one another. A Nassau is three matches in one. One point is given to the winner of the first nine holes; another point goes to the winner of the back nine; and a third point is given to the winner of the total 18 holes. As a general practice, points are converted into some type of compensation—cash, golf balls, etc.

Unlike tennis, golf has a great equalizer: the handicap system. A golfer's *handicap* simply is the number of strokes it would take him to reduce his average score to par. For instance, if you shoot an average score of 94 on a par 72 course, your handicap will be 22. As a result, when you are playing in formalized competition, usually at the club level, you generally will turn in two scores: a gross score, which is your overall total, and a net score, which is your overall total *minus* your handicap. So, if you are a 22-handicapper and happen to shoot a gross 87, your net score will be 65. And your friends will be calling you names behind your back.

Golf is a game with long-standing rules of etiquette. On greens, it's common courtesy to mark and remove a ball when it lies in the general path of an opponent's putt.

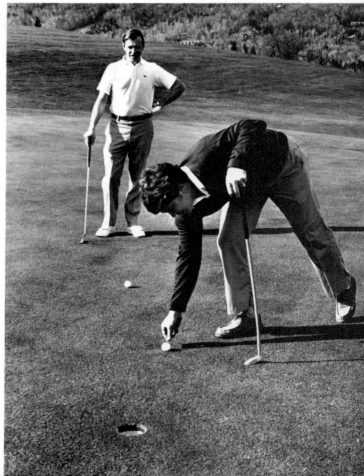

Holes are handicapped by degree of difficulty. The number 1 handicap hole is that hole that, on the average, plays to the highest score in relation to par. In this case, the par four, 425-yard twelfth is the number 1 handicap hole.

As for handicapping in match-play competition, each hole on a course is assigned a so-called severity rating—1 to 18. For example, say you are a 22-handicapper playing a 20-handicapper in the Class C club championship. The difference between your handicaps is two, which means that your opponent must give you two shots . . . "as they fall on the scorecard." So, look along the handicap line of the scorecard and circle the holes rated first and second in degree of difficulty. On each of these holes you get to subtract one stroke from your final score.

Equipment

Buying golf equipment—everything from clubs to balls to shoes to gloves—is a serious and expensive proposition, and one that is not made any easier by the hard-sell merchandising and marketing tactics practiced not only by equipment manufacturers, of which there are hundreds, but also by golf professionals, of which there are thousands. The standard top-line set of woods costs somewhere in the vicinity of $400, while the standard top-line set of irons costs somewhere between $500 and $600. Special-order sets of clubs can cost as much as $3,000. A good golf bag costs between $75 and $125, an average putter costs some $50, a pair of golf shoes—and what golfer has only one pair of shoes?—costs between $40 and $100, a golf glove costs about $10, and a package of three new golf balls costs more than $5. As you can see, this is a major investment. And even then your equipment will not approach the quality of the equipment used by most golf professionals.

Nowhere is the amateur player confronted with more mind-boggling and mouth-watering confusion than in the broad area of golf equipment. That's understandable. Like most people, golfers tend to be star-struck. So when the ten leading money winners on the pro golf tour

23

The metal wood (top) has become increasingly popular with golfers of all abilities, though many purists still prefer wood.

have sets of clubs that are produced by as many as eight different manufacturers, when those ten leading money winners play as many as six different makes of golf balls, and when those ten players use putters that look like everything from the kitchen sink to a zebra, the amateur golfer is ripe for the picking. And when the winner of some televised tournament happens to use some piece of equipment that nobody had ever seen before, well, that item immediately becomes the "in" thing in all golf. For instance, metal woods became very "in", and have certainly remained that way, when Jim Simon won the 1982 Crosby playing with new metal woods; Simon correctly told the TV audience that he hit the ball 20 and 30 yards longer with his metal woods. And when Jack Nicklaus won the 1986 Masters using a new Respone putter with a greatly oversized head, well, his company had 50,000 orders for that identical putter within the next two weeks.

But let's get down to the serious matters of selecting the right equipment for you and explaining the "in" language of the golf equipment business. When your friendly local pro tells you that you definitely need a certain set of forged-head graphites with 45 grams in the hosel and a swing weight of D-three, you should be able to say, "Sorry, pro, but I'd like a set of cast heads with stainless-steel shafts, 20 grams in the hosel, a swingweight of D-one, and grips over-

The variables in golf equipment are numerous, sometimes confusing. Trust your pro to fit you with a proper set of clubs.

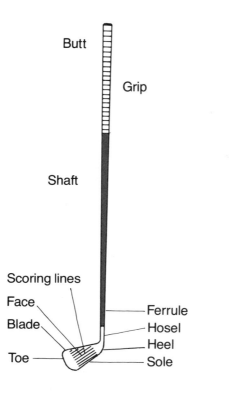

Anatomy of a club.

wrapped by one thirty-second. And I'd like the clubs to be one degree upright, too."

GOLF CLUBS

If you are serious about your game, purchase your clubs from a PGA golf professional. PGA pros are not just salespeople; they know what type of clubs you need to accommodate the peculiarities of your physique and—most importantly—of your swing, and may well have those exact clubs in stock. If not, they should be able to get clubs for you in a matter of days. Too many people, unfortunately, want their clubs *yesterday.* Considering that the average set of clubs lasts several seasons, having to wait a few days for the correct ones hardly seems unreasonable.

Sporting goods outlets also offer clubs for sale, but be wary of purchasing clubs in retail stores. As a rule, manufacturers peddle their top-line golf equipment only to golf pros—and sell their second-line clubs to department and discount stores. Also, salespeople in a retail store are seldom equipped to advise you properly on matters of club weight, length, and so on. Yes, you can save money by buying clubs from the big outlets, but if you go that route, be sure you know exactly what you want—and exactly what you are getting.

There was a major revolution in the golf industry during the 1980s as manufacturers turned to space age technology and developed a total new approach to the art of making golf clubs. What these manufacturers have done, in simple terms, is to make the meeting of golf club and golf ball a simpler and more productive event. They have done so by introducing the so-called metal wood and by refining the process of investment cast club making to the point where club faces now have reduced the margin of error to zero. No matter where you hit the ball on the face of an investment cast club—heel, toe, or dead square in the middle—the ball will take almost an identical flight.

Indeed, the Number 1 thing in golf huckstering these days is the matter of the club head's sweet spot. This is the percussion center, that point at which a club will not rotate when it is hit. It is the point of zero torque. In their endless efforts to make the game easier for the semi-skilled player—and, of course, to sell golf clubs—manufacturers have succeeded in expanding the sweet spot on a club head by spreading the weight throughout the head so that the golfer

A good sand wedge, for the average player, has a large flange.

supposedly can achieve maximum results no matter where on the face the ball is hit. The man given great credit for the creation of the so-called total life head is Karsten Solheim, the inventor of the hot-selling Ping golf clubs. While Ping clubs may not be cosmetically appealing, throughout the 1980s they were the Number 1 "in" thing in golf equipment. Some 50 percent of the players on the PGA Tour were using Pings regularly.

This, mind you, sparked considerable debate among the veterans on the Tour, many of whom felt quite strongly that the Pings and other type of investment-cast clubs made good golfers out of bad. In fact, with Pings and other investment cast clubs, the premium on skilled shotmaking is not as great as it is with the traditional forged-head clubs.

In fact, it is interesting to note that through 1987, although about 50 percent of the Tour pros used investment cast irons, only one such player, Bob Tway, who uses Pings, won a major championship—the 1986 PGA.

The bottom line is this: Investment cast clubs such as the Pings do indeed make golf an easier game to play. No matter where you hit the ball on the face of a Ping or one of its imitators, the ball will take the same flight. You can flat-out mishit the ball and still get productive results. So should you own such clubs? Put it this way: Pings and other investment cast clubs can very nicely correct all the errors in your swing.

What Clubs to Carry

The first question confronting the golfer is what clubs to carry. According to the rules of golf, you are permitted to have only fourteen clubs in your bag when playing in formal competition—everything from a club member-guest tournament to the U.S. Open. In tournaments, the penalty for playing with more than the allowed fourteen clubs is severe; in medal play it is two strokes per hole played prior to the discovery of the extra club(s) (to a maximum of four strokes), while in match play it is the loss of two holes (maximum) in a round.

In the old days, most golfers chose as their fourteen clubs four woods (numbers one through four or, by name, driver, brassie, spoon, and cleek), nine irons (a two-iron through a nine-iron, plus a wedge for short approach shots to the green and all sand-trap explosions), and a putter. Today, many touring professionals, as well as many low-handicap amateurs, carry only two woods in their bag (a driver and something between a No. 2½ and a No. 3½ wood specially made for them), along with eleven irons (a one-iron through a nine-iron plus a pitching wedge, equivalent in loft to a ten-iron, and a sand wedge), and, of course, a putter. Skilled golfers hit irons more precisely than they do

The hottest clubs in golf: Ping Eye-2s.

woods; semi-skilled or unskilled players—eager just to advance the ball—tend to be awed by long irons and feel more comfortable with a wood in their hands.

Regardless of your ability, forget about the two-wood, the brassie; it has become so obsolete that most manufacturers now produce it only on special order. Replace the two-wood in your bag with a sand wedge. This has become such a valuable club in the golfer's arsenal that many professionals would almost rather be caught without their driver than without their sand wedge.

The sand wedge can well be called the No. 1 stroke-saving club in any player's bag. It is not strictly for sand traps, either. It is the perfect club to use for those fifty-yards-and-in approach shots that must carry to the green on the fly because of ground-level hazards en route. A sand wedge also can be the perfect club for green-side recoveries from thick and wiry rough.

In selecting a sand wedge—most sets of irons do not include it as standard equipment—try to find one with a particularly large flange. The bigger the flange, the more bounce the sand wedge will have—and bounce is a major consideration when the golfer is faced with an explosion shot from a bunker.

As for your other clubs, the choice depends on your physical capabilities, your golfing skills, and your age. Strong, young (under thirty-five) golfers who play more than three rounds and practice on two or three other occasions each week are obviously well equipped to handle club loads similar to those of the touring professionals. On the other hand, the average amateurs—those once- or twice-a-week golfers whose handicaps range from 15 to infinity—must make concessions for their basic lack of ability and compose a club load that is best suited for *their* game—not the game of the touring pro.

The Irons

As a general rule, amateur golfers have less control over their long irons—everything from the one-iron, which also is a club that is not part of the standard set and must be specially ordered, to the four-iron—than they do over any other clubs in the bag. The longer irons—so called because of the distance they will send the ball—require strength and skill on the part of the player, mainly because of the relative sheerness of their faces. Also, most average golfers tend to play the golf course from tees placed in such a position that they are rarely faced with second shots requiring a long iron.

If you are not a low-handicap player, if you are not young and strong, and if you do not play golf several times a week, forget about carrying a one-iron and a two-iron, and perhaps a three-iron as well. Instead, consider the merits of the five-wood and maybe even the six-wood, both of which have become popular and effective clubs, as substitutes for those long irons that are so difficult to master.

Such thinking does not apply to low-handicap players. For them, the one-iron, two-iron, and three-iron can be lethal weapons once they have been mastered. The one-iron, for instance, is the perfect club to hit off the tee of a par-four hole that has a landing area surrounded by hazards; in fact, a well-struck one-iron should travel between 215 and 225 yards—or far enough that the player is not left with an impossible distance to the green, however distant it might be.

The rest of the irons—the five-iron through the pitching wedge—are elementary and necessary. There is no real substitute for any of them.

The Woods—or Metals

For the purposes of this discussion, the words "woods" and "metals" should be considered interchangeable. Of the woods or metals, the one-wood—the driver—is basic. Yet many golfers develop mental blocks about their drivers, becoming so perplexed that the club almost melts in their hands. It is a fear to be overcome, since in many ways the driver is the single most important club in your bag. Aside from the putter, it is generally the club used most often during a round. On the average course, which means an eighteen-hole layout with four par-three holes, you are called upon to hit what amounts to a drive on fourteen holes. The longer the tee shot on those par-four and par-five holes, the shorter the approach shot to the green. And the only way to hit "long" tee shots is to use a driver, a club which has an enormous head and a very sheer face. As such, it behooves all amateur golfers—regardless of skill level—to spend plenty of time on the practice tee learning how to hit their driver. Golf is a considerably easier game to play when you hit your tee shot 225 yards onto the fairway, rather than 170 yards into the rough.

In their desire to play the game with eleven irons, many pros and low-handicap amateurs have turned to a so-called bastard wood—something between a 2½ and a 3½—as the second piece of lumber in their bag. Because of their skills, honed on the practice tee, they can maneuver this club in such a way that it will give them the length they need to reach par-five holes with their second shot as well as the height they need to carry the ball over obstructions.

That may be fine for skilled players, but average amateurs should stick to the standard three- and four-woods, adding, if they wish, five- and six-woods as substitutes for a one-, two-, and three-iron.

As the specifications table on page 33 indicates, the five-wood has slightly more loft than a two-iron, and a considerably longer shaft. It also has a much bigger head. As a result, the average golfer should find it an easier club to hit. Also, the five-wood is less intimidating to look at than a two-iron, and it requires far less effort to swing. As for the six-wood, the average amateur player may well find that it serves more efficiently and more effectively than the three-iron and four-iron do. In any case, your local pro usually has such clubs as a five-wood and a six-wood available for testing—and you should try them out.

To sum up, the skilled player should think about carrying two woods—the driver and an approximation of a three-wood; eleven irons—everything from a one-iron to a nine-iron, plus a pitching wedge and a sand wedge; and a putter. The average amateur, though, should carry as many as five woods—driver, three-wood, four-wood, five-wood, and perhaps even a six-wood—and compensate for the overload of woods by carrying only eight irons—four-iron through nine-iron, plus pitching wedge and sand wedge—in addition to the putter.

Lie

The next step in the club selection process is finding the proper specifications for your particular swing and your particular physique. Without a doubt, the

A club has the proper lie if, at address, the club head rests squarely on the ground (middle) the toe should not be pointed up (top), or down (bottom).

most important consideration is the "lie" of the club. In technical terms, the lie is the angle between the club's hosel—the socket for the shaft—and the head. Or, to put it another way, the lie is how the golf club sits when you hold it in the address position. At address, the blade of your club must rest squarely on the ground. If it does not rest that way—if it sits either on its toe or on its heel —then you will immediately be in a no-win situation; you will be forced to alter the proper pattern of your swing in order to get the club head back into a position from which it can strike the ball squarely.

Lie is basically an individual matter relating to a golfer's physique and preferred position at address. It is imperative that a player have clubs that are the proper lie. An improper lie—the club's sole not resting flat—creates an improper angle of the club face at impact, which will greatly influence the direction of the shot. For instance, a tall person—anyone over, say, six feet— who holds the hands properly high will stand much closer to the ball at address than a short person. As such, tall golfers might well need clubs with a more upright lie—maybe by as many as 2 degrees. Short golfers, on the other hand, might well need a flatter lie in their clubs.

Length

This raises another question: Do tall golfers need longer clubs than short golfers? The answer is "maybe." Just because you happen to be six feet five inches, you don't necessarily need clubs that are longer than the standard length. And if you happen to be five feet six inches, you may well want clubs longer than standard length in order to develop a bigger arc in your swing. Sound strange? Tom Weiskopf, who stands six foot three, uses clubs that are half an inch shorter than the standard length, while Gary Player, who is about five-seven, uses clubs that are an inch longer than the standard length.

How, then, do you determine what is the proper length for your clubs? It depends on how far your fingertips are from the ground when they hang naturally at your side. Weiskopf, for instance, has very long arms, while Player has short ones; in fact, Weiskopf's arms come to rest perhaps half a finger closer to the ground than Player's. So forget about how tall or short you are. If you are long-armed, you can play with standard-length clubs—or you may need clubs shorter than standard length. On the other hand, if you are short-armed, you will probably need clubs slightly longer than standard length.

Again, the one person who can expertly advise you on all these matters of lie and length is your PGA professional.

The following chart lists the specifications for standard clubs provided by most manufacturers:

Club	Degree of Loft	Degree of Lie	Men's Length	Women's Length
One-wood	11	55	43"	42"
Two-wood	14	55¼	42½"	41½"
Three-wood	16	55½	42"	41"
Four-wood	19	55¾	41½"	40½"
Five-wood	21	56	41"	40"
One-iron	17	55	39"	38"
Two-iron	20	56	38½"	37½"
Three-iron	23	57	38"	37"
Four-iron	27	58	37½"	36½"
Five-iron	31	59	37"	36"
Six-iron	35	60	36½"	35½"
Seven-iron	39	61	36"	35"
Eight-iron	43	62	35½"	34½"
Nine-iron	47	63	35"	34"
Pitching wedge	51	63	35"	34"
Sand wedge	56	63	35"	34"

The Head

Lie and length aside, one of the major equipment problems confronting the modern golfer is the matter of the club head. In the old days, golfers had little choice; manufacturers—and there weren't that many—offered only a very limited selection of club-head designs, and golfers had to take them or leave them. As a result, the general rule was to look for a set of clubs that "looked good"—and use them until they wore out. Today, though, club heads are a subject of endless discussion.

Basically, all irons have either cast heads or forged heads. In the investment cast process, metal is poured into preformed molds that have the scoring lines and the stampings contained in them—and ultimately a finished club is produced. In the forged process, the raw head is individually hand filed and ground into a finished product by a skilled craftsman. Cast heads are fine for the average amateur golfer, but the low-handicap amateur might well want to invest in a set of the forged variety. Most tour players prefer forged to cast heads; forged heads tend to be softer and thus provide a better feel, and they are easier to bend if the player wants to make modifications.

Woods, of course, are shaped from various kinds of wood—and now, metal. The best wood heads are made from persimmon. Many manufacturers offer inserts—that part of the face of a wood that is centered in the middle of the club face—made of aluminum or plastic or various types of glass, as well as wood. One of the newer insert materials is something called Gamma Fine, a wood product that provides greater distance to shots because of its greater recovery characteristics. The metal head has no insert; it is one solid piece of metal shaped into the form of the desired club.

A club is the proper length if, when held at address, the head rests flat on the ground.

Cast club heads come from the mold rough. They are then ground and polished by hand.

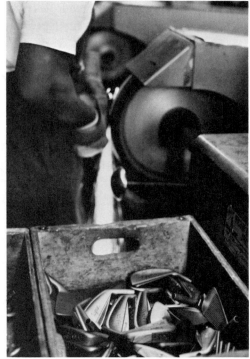

Built-in Faces

In recent years, manufacturers have designed wood clubs with built-in hook faces or built-in slice faces simply by angling the club head on the shaft, i.e., closing or opening the club head, respectively. The sales pitches for these gimmicky clubs are obvious. Are you slicing the ball too much? Well, buy a set of our hook-faced woods and you'll stop slicing overnight. Are you hooking your shots too much? Buy a set of our slice-faced clubs and you'll stop hooking overnight. And, of course, if you're hitting the ball dead straight all the time but would like to start hitting hooks or slices, why not buy a set of clubs with a built-in hook or slice?

Here's why not. At address, the face of the club must be set squarely at the target or the golfer will need to make in-swing alterations in order to have the club head hit the golf ball squarely. With a hook-faced club, the face will be lined up well to the left of the target at address, while with a slice-faced club the face will be lined up well to the right of the target at address. All those wrongs will not produce a good shot. So skip the gimmicks.

The Shaft

The other part of the golf club that has been treated to major technical change and improvement in recent years is the shaft, although all too often the benefits of these advancements have been lost in the profusion of explanations extolling their wonders. The first true discovery in the area of shafts was steel, which replaced the hickory used in the clubs played by most of golf's early-day legends, right up through Bobby Jones. Then, in the late 1950s and early 1960s, many manufacturers flooded the market with clubs featuring both aluminum and fiberglass, instead of steel, and simultaneously spewed forth loud pronouncements about the advantages—longer drives, straighter drives—offered by these "revolutionary" new shafts. Unfortunately for the manufacturers, these clubs proved to be about as popular as the Edsel. For one thing, they both lacked the harsh *click-click* sound that steel seemed to impart at impact. For another, they both seemed to lack the whippiness that steel shafts had in varying degrees.

After this period of experimentation, club makers went back to stainless steel for their shafts until the late 1960s, when graphite shafts suddenly began to infiltrate the market. Not only was graphite considerably lighter than steel, by at least an ounce per shaft, but also its fibers could be arranged in the direction of stresses developed in the shaft—all of which meant that graphite

A graphite club gets its strength and "whip" from the graphite fibers wrapped the length of the shaft and stabilized in a hard-setting resin.

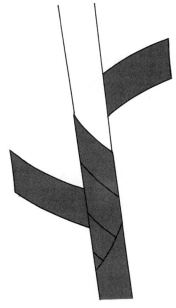

seemed to offer greater efficiency than stainless steel. Put simply, the golfer developed more club-head speed with graphite than stainless steel, and the end result was extra distance.

On the heels of graphite shafts came graphite shafts combined with the element boron, which supposedly helped reduce the weight of the shafts by still another half an ounce; after that came titanium shafts, which were reported to be almost 50 percent lighter than stainless steel. And, of course, the lighter the shaft, the greater the speed of the club head at impact—and the longer the ball travels.

Then, as now, these graphite-, graphite-with-boron-, and titanium-shafted clubs cost three to five times more than stainless-steel-shafted ones; a full set of titanium costs approximately $3,000, and a complete set of graphites costs more than $2,000, while a set of top-line clubs with stainless-steel shafts costs about $800. As a result, it is hardly surprising that these ultra-modern shafts did not take over the market. However, many golfers, including a large number

Shafts are marked for flexibility. Have your pro help select the right flex for your swing.

of touring professionals, do use drivers that have graphite shafts. The driver, of course, is usually the club employed most frequently during a round, and distance—particularly *extra* distance—off the tee is critical. As such, the expense may well be worthwhile.

The problem with all these new shafts is that they demand a modified swing pattern, one that is slightly slower and less whippy than the swing employed for other clubs. Such a modification is not easy to achieve, particularly by the stronger player intent upon attacking the golf ball with power and might in perfect harness. However, for the senior golfer and the player who does not have great physical strength, the benefit—*extra* distance—provided by these ultra-modern shafts is well worth whatever compensations must be made in the swing.

But all things considered, the best shaft for most amateur golfers still is stainless steel, which provides plenty of variation in both feel and action. For instance, the so-called dynamic shafts have their "kick" at the bottom and thus tend to launch the ball sharply and quickly upward. In the so-called pro-pel shafts, on the other hand, the source of the action is much closer to the handle of the club.

Shaft Flexibility

The basic rules in determining the proper shaft flexibility are these:

1. If you are an older man or a very strong woman, use an A shaft, which is rather whippy and will help you produce greater club-head speed.

2. If you are the average woman golfer, you should use an L shaft, which is the standard women's shaft.

3. If you are an average male golfer, you should use an R shaft, the regular shaft which is a cross between stiff and whippy.

4. If you are a strong male golfer, someone who plays regularly and competitively, you should use a stiff or an extra-stiff shaft.

Once again, your club pro is well qualified to offer advice on all these matters.

The Grip

Next, there is the grip of the club. There are two decisions to be made here: (1) what type of grip you should have on your clubs, and (2) how big in diameter your grips should be.

For the most part, grips tend to fall into two categories, leather or rubber. Neither grip seems to offer any greater advantage to the player; about half the pros, both men and women, use leather grips—that is, genuine calf—and about half use rubber ones. It all becomes a matter of personal preference, with "feel" usually being the ultimate determinant. Leather grips do require more maintenance than the all-weather rubber composition grips and cost about twice as much. For those reasons, if nothing else, all-weather rubber grips would seem to be ideal for amateurs—those who play mainly on weekends. Whatever grips you use, once they become too hard and lose their tractability—their tackiness—replace them immediately. Otherwise your clubs will fly out of your hands and into orbit during your swing.

The standard diameter of the grip can be altered quite easily—made bigger or smaller—to make allowances for the size of the particular player's hands. Players with big hands may well want their grips built up by 1/32nd or even 1/16th of an inch, while players with small hands may want the diameter of their grips reduced by some fraction of an inch; a pro shop attendant can do this quite simply by adding to or subtracting from the normal wrappings around the top of the shaft, under the grip, until the desired thickness has been reached.

Some pros prefer the leather grip (left), but the most popular and most functional grip is rubber composition (right).

It is vitally important that the golfer develop a solid "feel" between the hands and the grip—and ultimately, of course, the complete club. The grip must feel comfortable in the player's hands and it must be fairly secure, not too tight but not too loose.

One word of caution. A wrong grip size often will lead to erratic shots. For instance, if the grip is much too thin, the inherent looseness will tend to accelerate the closing of the club face and produce too much of an unwanted hook. If the grip is much too big, the inherent tightness will tend to decelerate the closing of the club face and produce an unwanted fade. Again, check out your grip size with your club pro.

Swing Weight

Now that we have assembled the "right" club for your swing and your physique, the only question remaining to be answered is the matter of the proper swing weight. The swing weight of a club is an intricate calculation that is translated into a simple letter-number designation; the formula is based on a computation called the ounce-inch ratio and relates the weight of the grip end of the club to its head weight. Put simply, the higher the swing weight, the heavier the club head will feel to the player—and the heavier the club itself most likely will be.

Unless you are unusually muscular and powerful, you should use clubs with a basically standard swing weight; for women and for older men, this is something in the high Cs, while for most men it is usually D-1 or D-2. Strong women golfers may well want to use clubs with a swing weight of D-0 or even D-1, while strong male golfers may want to use clubs with a swing weight as high as D-6.

As always, consult your club pro as to the correct swing weight for your clubs.

Club Care

Golf clubs represent a major capital investment, so you should keep your clubs in good repair at all times.

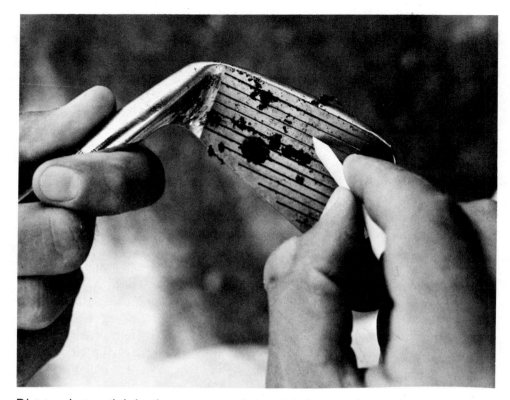

Dirt tends to stick in the grooves of the club face and can alter the course of a shot, so keep your grooves clean by taking a tee to them.

On the course, always carry a towel on your bag and wipe off the face of your clubs before you use them. Specks of dirt tend to lodge in the grooves, and these impediments can directly affect the flight of the golf ball. At the end of the round, either you or your caddie should wash your irons and clean your woods with a special solution that golf pros always have available in their bag room.

Never leave your clubs outdoors at night, and when you store them, set them in a horizontal—not vertical—position. This helps prevent warping. Also, always keep covers on your woods; they help preserve the finish of the clubs.

Club care is very important; not only do clean clubs make you a better golfer, they also eliminate the need for buying new clubs every two or three years. There are professionals on the men's and women's tours who have played with the same woods and irons for more than a decade.

If some manufacturers of golf balls had their way, every 32-handicap duffer in the world would regularly hit 400-yard drives, and some players would never lose a ball hit into the rough; one company recently put on the market a golf ball with a beeping device implanted in it, so the golfer could easily track it down. Fortunately for the game, however, the United States Golf Association, in conjunction with the Royal and Ancient Golf Club of St. Andrews, has set rigid standards to which all golf balls must conform—or else be declared illegal for competitive play. No beeper balls, please.

There are dozens of high-quality—and legal—golf balls available to the player, and at a wide range of prices—and colors. In essence, the four decisions confronting you in the matter of golf ball selection are: (1) What type of cover do you want? (2) How much compression do you want? (3) What trajectory do you want your shots to reach? (4) How much do you want to pay?

Dimple configuration largely determines the trajectory of a golf ball. The deep, small dimples on the ball at the left ensure a long, low flight while the shallower, larger dimples on the ball in the center give the ball terrific lift. The ball at right weds an equal number of both configurations. The correct choice is largely a matter of wind conditions and personal preference.

Cover

For years, most golf balls had a balata cover, which cuts fairly easily when the club head does not make proper contact with the ball at impact—or, in other words, when the leading edge of the blade hits the ball in the wrong place. Once this soft-covered ball acquires what golfers jokingly call a "smile," it is barely fit for play; the aperture in the cover not only limits the distance the ball travels but also causes the ball to take an erratic flight.

Then, in the 1960s, Du Pont shook up the golf ball industry when it produced a hard plastic composition cover for golf balls called Surlyn. As a result, the hard Surlyn-covered balls became an instant hit—and remain so—among those players who are not pure strikers of the golf ball; instead of having to switch to a brand new golf ball every few holes, these players are able to use the same ball for two or three rounds. The major flaw of Surlyn-covered balls, though, is that, while they do not cut, the cover does peel—and consequently they can be difficult to putt because the peeling edges directly affect the roll of the ball. One other problem with Surlyn-covered balls is that they do not make an audible *click* when the club head meets the ball; in fact, Surlyn-covered balls produce no discernible sound when they are struck. For these reasons, not many skilled golfers use Surlyn-covered balls on a regular basis.

Surlyn covers come in different thicknesses too, and the thicker the cover, the farther the ball will fly when struck by an iron because the center of gravity is more to the outside of the ball. Because of this phenomenon of physics, most touring professionals always used to switch from a balata-covered ball to a Surlyn-covered—or solid—ball whenever they played a long par-three hole that required a well-struck iron shot off the tee. However, in 1979, the USGA and the Royal and Ancient issued an official communiqué that outlawed this practice; now, all tournament players, both amateur and professional, can use only one model of golf ball during an entire round.

In general, the best recommendation regarding golf ball selection is this: If you are a low-handicap player, and/or one who engages in serious competition, you should use a balata-covered ball, but if you are only a weekend player, why not economize and use a Surlyn-covered ball.

Whatever type of ball you play, though, don't use it for 18 holes each round. Golf balls do get beaten down and need time to recover. Always have two golf balls at your disposal, and alternate them on a regular basis—every other hole, say, or every third hole.

Compression

A golf ball's compression is a measurement of the hardness of the ball. The common belief among most amateur golfers is that the greater the compression, the farther the ball will travel. While this may well be true, it is also true that the greater the compression, the tougher it is to compress it. Almost all touring pros use 100-compression golf balls, and so do most top-level amateur players, as well they should. However, the best ball for the weekend player, the once-a-week golfer, is one with a compression of about 90. In most cases, the stated compression of a golf ball is a round figure because manufacturers cannot possibly produce golf balls with a uniform compression. Just remember that only the more skilled players can effectively handle a ball with a compression of 100.

Trajectory

The trajectory of a golf ball is a matter of dimple configuration; dimples determine the ball's flight. Basically, the deeper and the smaller the dimples, the longer and lower the ball will travel, while with shallower and larger dimples, a ball will travel higher. Just as they frequently switched from balata- to Surlyn-covered balls on long par-three holes, touring pros and top-level amateur players also switched to balls with larger, shallower dimples on those holes when the wind was at their backs. The larger, shallower dimples would help lift the ball practically into orbit immediately after impact, and the ball

On a wound ball, (left) the ball's compression is determined by the tightness of the elastic windings around the center of the ball.

On a solid ball (right), there essentially is no compression measurement; the relative hardness of the cover determines distance.

would get caught in the wind and travel great distances. This situation dismayed both the USGA and the Royal and Ancient, and in 1979 a ruling was made that players could not switch from one dimple configuration to another during a round. On the whole, the best dimple configuration would appear to be the old-style one with deeper and smaller dimples, not the shallower and larger dimples.

Cost

How much you spend for a golf ball is a personal matter. The serious golfer should purchase the top-of-the-line make of ball, which now sells for about $1.75. However, the less serious player can purchase serviceable golf balls for between 75 cents and $1.75.

A microscopic blip of dirt can directly alter the flight of a ball, so use the ball washer located on most tees and use it often. And be sure to dry off the ball, because water also can hinder the flight of a shot.

Gloves

Do you need a golf glove? Yes.

Almost all pros on the men's and women's tours wear gloves on their leading hand—the leading hand being the left hand for right-handed golfers and the right hand for left-handed golfers. The palm of a glove tends to become tacky and thus enables the golfer to obtain a more secure grip on the club with what is normally the weaker hand. Also, gloves naturally help eliminate the problem of developing calluses on the hand. However, most pros do not wear their gloves when they are putting because they want to get as much feel into the putt as possible. A glove, they believe, reduces the amount of feel between the putter and the hands.

A golf glove is a must for a firm, secure grip on the club.

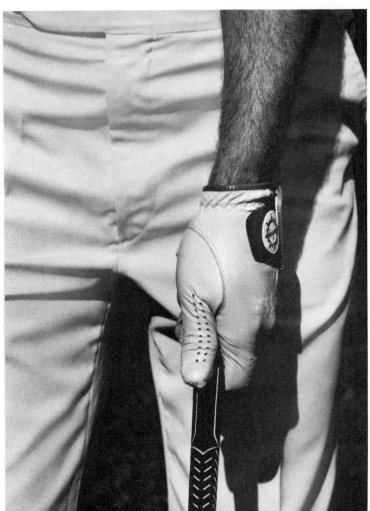

Shoes

Are spiked golf shoes a necessary expense? Absolutely!

Golf shoes are as important as golf clubs. The spikes on the bottom of the shoes permit you to take a firm, solid stance no matter where you happen to be, on or off the course. Too, the spikes serve to aerate the greens. Like golf clubs and golf balls, the spikes must be kept free of impediments—particularly chunks of dirt and grass that tend to clog the spikes in the middle and cause golfers to slip during their swing.

Don't—repeat, don't—ever use ripple-soled shoes when you play golf. They do not settle into the greens and tend to leave them looking very bumpy and choppy. While that may not bother the wearer of ripple-soled shoes, it will bother the next golfer who has to putt over the hills and valleys left by the ripples.

Keep your spikes clean. Grass and dirt can clog the spikes of your shoes and prevent you from taking a solid stance.

3

The Grip

A fundamentally sound and solid grip is the foundation upon which the entire golf swing is built. After all, if you hold the golf club the wrong way, how can you possibly expect to hit the golf ball with consistency? You can't. Oh, perhaps you will strike an occasional good shot, but the bad shots will far outnumber the good ones. The grip is the ignition system for the engine. The grip makes the golf swing work—or not work.

The golf world is littered with players who had aspirations of becoming big winners on the pro tours but were forced back into obscurity because they had basic flaws in their grips. As one established touring pro says, "It's one thing to be able to play with a bad grip on some wide-open cow pasture back home, but it's another thing to try to play with that bad grip on some of the tight championship courses where major tournaments are held. Bad grips have ruined many golf careers. You just cannot survive with a bad grip, it's that simple."

51

A firm, fundamentally sound grip is the most basic element in your game.

TYPES OF GRIP

Basically, there are three types of grip—overlapping, interlocking, and baseball. Each is fundamentally correct, and each has been used with great success by different players on the tours. For example, Jack Nicklaus and Tom Watson employ different grips—Nicklaus prefers the interlocking grip, while Watson uses the overlapping grip—but the dissimilarities between their grips obviously have not affected their shot-making performances or their money winnings.

As is the case in so many technical areas of the golf swing, the ultimate determinant regarding the type of grip you should employ is a matter of personal choice. Over a period of time, one particular grip will begin to feel more or less comfortable than another, and as a result it will soon begin to provide better or worse results with your shots. So experiment with each of the three basic types—and then decide which grip is the best grip for you.

The overlapping grip is the most popular way to hold the club because it offers the best combination of strength and feel.

The Overlapping Grip

The overlapping grip, also known as the Vardon grip—named after the late Harry Vardon, the brilliant English shot maker who was the Nicklaus of the early days of the twentieth century—is the grip favored by the great majority of players. More importantly, it is the suggested grip for a player who has big hands or strong hands—or both. With this grip, the little finger of the right hand overlaps the index finger of the left hand and sort of rests on the closure between the index finger and the middle finger of the left hand.

The Interlocking Grip

The interlocking grip, which someday will probably be known as the Nicklaus grip, is suggested for a player with small hands or weak hands—or both—

The interlocking grip is best for players with small or weak hands because it provides a stronger hold on the club.

54

The baseball grip is best for older and infrequent golfers because it provides maximum feel and hand action.

Art Wall, Jr., who has made more than forty holes in one, now favors the grip used by— well, Wade Boggs.

because it makes possible a stronger hold on the club. With the interlocking grip, the little finger of the right hand is set firmly between the index finger and the middle finger of the left hand. Or, to say it another way, the index finger of the left hand is set firmly between the last two fingers of the right hand.

The Baseball Grip

The baseball grip is an ideal grip for older players, weaker players, and those who play golf only once or twice a year—as on an annual company outing. However, this is not to say it is a grip that should be shunned by better players; Bob Rosburg, the TV golf announcer, enjoyed a highly successful career on the pro tour while playing with a baseball grip. There is no interlocking or overlapping with the baseball grip; instead, the index finger of the left hand and the little finger of the right hand snuggle against each other, and the thumb of the left hand is set squarely down the middle of the shaft. To this day Rosburg maintains that the baseball grip provides the maximum feel and the maximum hand action possible during the swing.

GRIPPING THE CLUB

Gripping the club itself is not a casual thing. The hands must feel both firm and comfortable as they hold the club; there cannot be any tension or looseness, any forced effort at any time.

To grip the club properly, first set it on the ground so that the club head rests in its natural soled position with the face of the club set dead square to the target. One common flaw among many amateur golfers is that they take their club from the caddie or yank it from the bag on their golf cart and then apply their overlapping, interlocking, or baseball grip while holding the club in midair. The face of the club could be closed or opened or even turned backward, for all they know. Then, many times, they simply walk over to their ball, put the club head down behind it, and flail away. (After that, they usually walk into the woods to look for it.)

Only with the club head resting on the ground and the club face set square to the target—meaning that it is in direct line with the target—are you ready to apply your grip. And whatever grip you use, it is imperative that the back of your top or lead hand and the palm of your bottom hand both are set squarely at your target.

56 **Gripping the club.** Take the club with your top hand first, resting the butt of the club in your palm, atop the pad at the point where the last two fingers meet (A).

The rest of your top hand should then fall naturally into position (B).

Next, wrap your bottom hand around the club so that the club rests against your fingers—not against your palm (C).

Put the rest of your hand around the club (D).

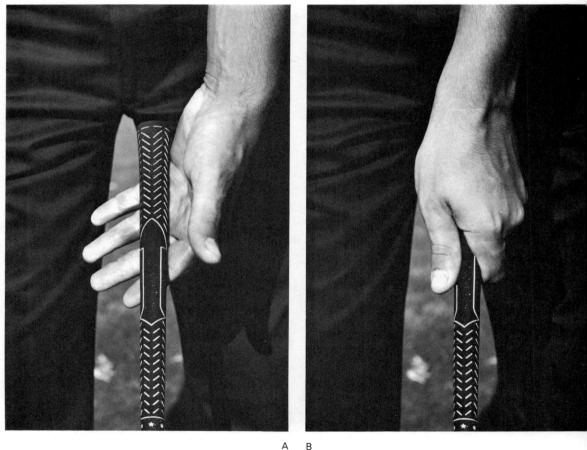

A   B

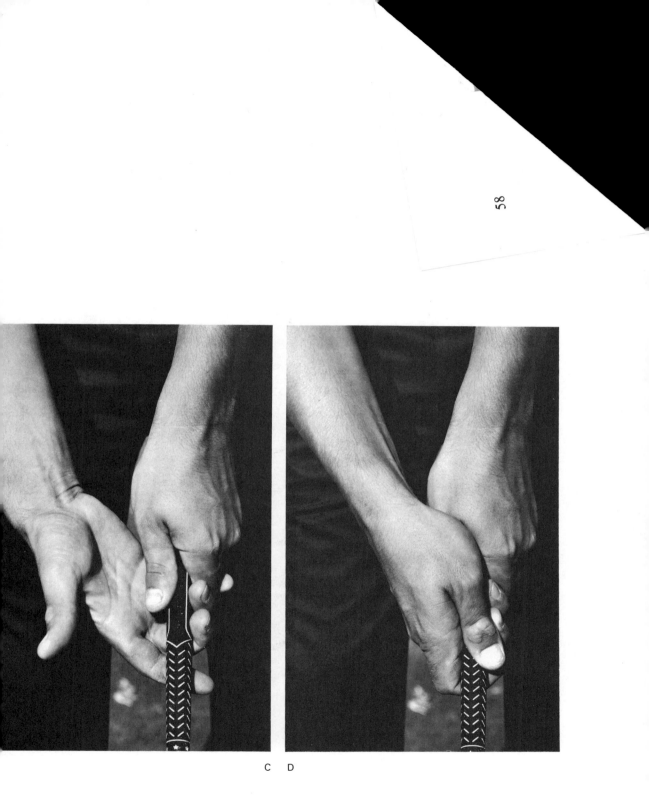

C   D

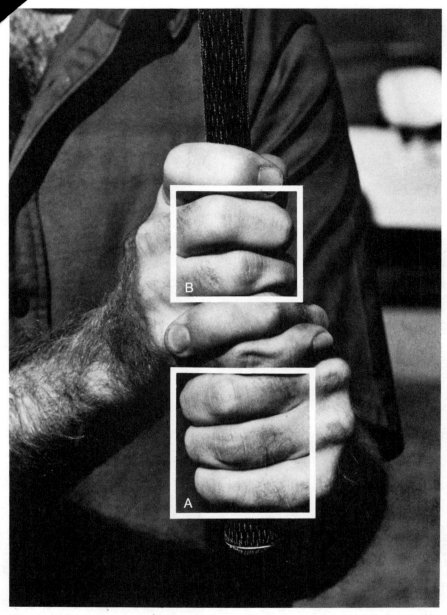

The last three fingers of the top hand (box A) and the middle and ring fingers of the lower hand (box B) should exert most of the pressure in the grip.

Take the club with your top hand first. The butt end of the club should rest in your palm, atop the pad at the point where the last two fingers begin. Once the butt end is in place, the rest of the top part of the club should fall naturally into position across the base of the middle and the index fingers. The thumb of the top hand should be set squarely down the center of the shaft.

Now wrap the bottom hand around the club, doing this in such a way that the club rests against your fingers, not against your palm. As for the position of the thumb of the bottom hand, make certain that the thumb and index finger of the bottom hand touch each other ever so gently once they are in place. This gentle touch is one of the checkpoints you should use to determine if your grip position is correct.

Once you have the club wrapped in your overlapping or interlocking or baseball grip, don't strangle it. Too many amateur golfers operate on the theory that the golf club must be held very tightly. Not so. Golf is not a game of white knuckles. Try to hold the club in such a way that it feels like a normal extension of your hands. How do you hold a pencil? Firmly, but not too firmly. How do you open a door? Well, you don't grab the knob and wrench it off. So don't squeeze the grip of your golf club either. The important thing is to grip the golf club tightly enough so that you will control the club throughout the swing in a natural, not forced, way. If you do strangle the club, you will interrupt the transfer of power throughout your body.

In holding the club, the last three fingers of the top hand apply most of the pressure, while the thumb and index finger of the top hand sort of tag along for a free ride. As for the bottom hand, the middle and ring fingers exert the most pressure in their roles as the anchors that keep the bottom hand in proper position, while the index finger and the thumb provide minor pressure support; the little finger gets a free ride.

As for the hands themselves, they should apply pressure equally, and remain unitized at all times.

During the swing, the top hand will naturally exert more and more pressure as it fulfills its role of leading and controlling the direction—the path—of the club. The pressure applied by the bottom hand should remain at a constant level throughout the swing. In terms of total pressure, each hand should supply an equal amount on the grip. When the balance of pressure gets out of sync, the result will be a bad swing—and, of course, a bad shot. Too much pressure by the bottom hand will produce both a fast swing and an overswing, while too much pressure by the top hand will tend to keep the club from reaching its regular high point on the backswing.

It is important that you think of your two hands as being one single unit, ι independent parts with separate roles. In line with this thinking, remember at there should be no "open spaces" within your grip. For reasons of personal ɔmfort, many golfers tend to let the index finger of their bottom hand—the so-called trigger finger—separate from the rest of the grip unit and take a solitary position perhaps two finger-widths lower on the shaft. By doing this, they create a gap in the unit—and a flaw in the grip. Also, some golfers who employ the baseball grip tend to separate their hands by an inch or so as they hold the golf club. This is fine if, as they say in baseball, you want to bunt the ball. But home-run hitters don't separate their hands on the bat handle—and you should not separate your hands on the golf grip. Fingers and hands together, please.

Shortening Up on the Handle

As they grip the club, those amateur golfers who are not interested in hitting the ball alongside the Nicklauses and the Watsons and the Zoellers—and who want more control—ought to think about shortening up on the handle of the grip, much like many baseball players—particularly singles and doubles hitters —shorten up on the bat handle. In golf, as in baseball, not everyone is equipped to swing for the fences each time up. In golf, as in baseball, the real trick is to make good contact with every swing. Golfers, like baseball players, don't want to hit foul balls—or, worse still, strike out.

So if you're not built like a home-run hitter, choke every golf club at least one inch down the shaft for normal shots and as many as three or four inches for all finesse-type approach shots to the green. The golf club is essentially an extension of your arms; in effect, you are hitting the golf ball with your arms. By shortening up on the grip, you will swing the club with much more control. Think of it this way. The golf club is really a utensil. When is the last time you operated a 43-inch bottle opener? By shortening up, you will not strike out so often.

Of course, shortening up on the grip also will reduce the distance that the ball will travel. To compensate for a choked-up grip, simply go one club lower than you normally would hit for each shot. For instance, rather than take out a five-iron, hold it at the end of the shaft, and then try to smash the shot 170 yards to the green, take out a four-iron instead, choke down on the grip, and then hit a firm, solid shot for the same 170 yards.

Unfortunately, there are some golfers who think that shortening up on the

Shortening up on the grip is a good way to improve the control of your club. Result: better accuracy.

grip is a confession of weakness or old age. That's nonsense. Check out the batting averages in the major leagues. Of the top twenty hitters in baseball, perhaps fifteen qualify as singles and doubles hitters who shorten up on the bat handle. And the golf tour is filled with players who'd rather "bunt" a four-iron 170 yards onto the green than "home-run" a five-iron 170 yards into the woods.

The Vs

In the old days, the Vs—that is, the areas formed by your thumbs and index fingers as they grip the club—were considered the most controversial part of the grip. There were pros who taught that the Vs must point to your back shoulder, or else you'd hit every shot into the right woods. There were pros who said that the Vs must point to your front shoulder, or else you'd hit every shot into the left woods. And there were other pros who said that the Vs must point

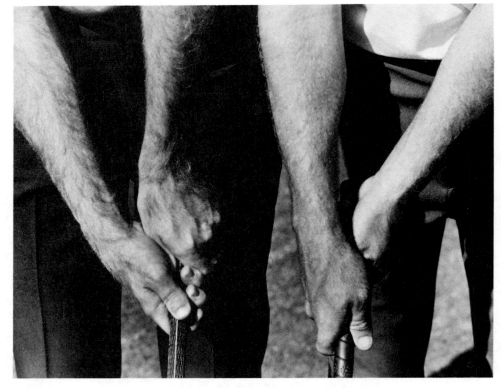

How not to hold the club: The grip at the left is much too "strong," the grip at the right much too "weak."

to your chin, your navel, your nose, your mouth, your ears, your hip, or even your eyes. In those days, too, golf instructors taught that players should use a "strong" grip or a "weak" grip—the suggested grip being the one employed by the instructor.

The "Strong" Grip

In assuming a "strong" grip, also known as a hook grip, on the club, the golfer does not set the thumb of the top hand down the center of the shaft; instead, the entire top hand is set slightly to the rear side of the shaft and then the bottom hand is fitted into place. As a result, the back of the top hand and the palm of the bottom hand will face skyward—not in the direction of the target —and the Vs of the grip will point sharply in the direction of the golfer's right shoulder. The "strong" grip ultimately leads to a right-to-left flight of the golf ball—or left-to-right for left-handed players—but all too often the player does not have the skill to control the hooking pattern of the ball.

The "Weak" Grip

The grip advocated in this chapter resembles the so-called "weak" grip. check the positioning of the Vs in the grip suggested here, you will notic they point in the direction of your lead shoulder, not your back shoulder. More importantly, the back of the lead hand and the palm of the bottom hand both are set squarely at the target. This grip may be called the "weak" grip, but it offers the best possible chance to hit the golf ball solidly—and in such a way that you will be able to control its flight.

Summary Checkpoints

- Take your grip when the club is resting naturally on the ground.
- Set the back of your top hand and the palm of your bottom hand squarely at the target.
- Don't strangle the club.
- The two hands must work as one.
- Shorten up on the grip.

Keep Your Hands Clean

In a recent U.S. Open, one of the amateur qualifiers suddenly turned what looked to be a good birdie possibility on a par-five hole into a disastrous triple-bogey eight by shanking his third shot into a ditch. After his round, the player offered what seemed to be a curious explanation for that shanked shot. While trying to figure out how to play the fifty-yard pitch shot onto the green, he said that he scratched his head several times and got what he called "greasy kid stuff" all over his right hand. As a result, he lost control of the club during his backswing and hit the shank into the ditch.

When playing golf you must keep your hands as clean as possible. Golf pros, for instance, never shake hands with their friends or admirers during a round; they don't want to risk the possibility of having their hands come into contact with foreign substances. Who knows? Maybe the handshaker just spilled cola or syrup or sun lotion. Or just scratched his head.

Always carry a towel on your golf bag, and every six or seven holes dip one end of the towel into water. That way, if your hands get sticky, you'll be able to wipe them clean.

4

The Swing

As any professional golfer will admit, there is no such thing as a perfect golf swing. Some people, for instance, describe Arnold Palmer's swing as a lurch—or even a swipe. According to the critics, Ben Hogan's swing was too flat, Byron Nelson's swing was too fast and too upright, and Bobby Jones's swing was too slow and had a loop at the top. As for Lee Trevino, the critics like to joke that the merry Mexican borrowed his swing from a caddie and sets up in such a way that it looks as though he's going to hit a shank every time. On the other hand, Tom Watson seems to have a textbook swing, one that he appears to repeat by the numbers, but the critics stubbornly maintain that Watson sometimes speeds up his swing tempo under pressure.

Perhaps the least flawed of all golf swings belongs to Sam Snead, whose every move over the golf ball is graceful and smoothly effortless. Indeed, if any player deserves the title of Sweet Swinging, it is Sammy. But Snead has always played with a hook grip, a strong grip—and some critics insist that you cannot have a perfect swing if you have a strong grip. So there you are!

In developing a swing, the worst thing you can do is flat-out copy the swing of some other

Perfect form: Everything is in place as Seve Ballesteros tracks his ball at the completion of a shot.

player. It is, of course, one thing to incorporate a certain aspect of some legendary player's swing as part of your own, but it is another matter to pattern your whole swing after someone else's. What works for Nicklaus or Palmer or Snead or Watson simply may not work for you. People are built differently—physically as well as mentally—and as a result they must find their own way. In time, that way may well prove to be the best.

Develop your own swing by properly executing its fundamental components in a style that is yours and yours alone. The trick is to reach the point of impact, where the club head makes contact with the ball, at that exact moment when everything in the swing is in perfect position. Indeed, Nicklaus and Snead may have swings that are visibly and markedly different, but at the point of impact they are locked into a position that is strikingly similar in every way.

There are three basic types of stance: open, closed, and square.

The Open Stance

With an open stance, your lead foot (left foot for right-handed golfers, right foot for left-handed golfers) is set away from the ball so that it rests a few inches behind a line drawn through the toe of your back foot and parallel to the line of flight.

The open stance is a control stance and produces a shot that moves from left to right—a fade—because it restricts the amount of shoulder, body, and hip

Three stances. The open stance (far left), with the left foot turned out to the left, encourages a swing that will produce a left-to-right flight of the ball; the closed stance (center), with the left foot pointed to the right of the target, encourages a swing that will produce a right-to-left flight of the ball. The square stance (right), with both feet and the club all aligned squarely at the target, is the stance for most golf shots.

turn you can make during the swing and creates an outside-to-inside swing plane.

The Closed Stance

With the closed stance, your back foot is set away from the ball so that it rests a few inches behind a line drawn through the toe of your lead foot and parallel to the line of flight. The stance qualifies as a hook stance because it tends to produce a roundhouse type of inside-to-outside swing at the ball. Both the open and the closed stances serve a definite purpose, though, when you are faced with a shot that requires a pronounced left-to-right or right-to-left movement of the ball.

The Square Stance

For the most part, the correct stance for you is the square stance. With this stance, both feet are placed evenly so that a line drawn between the toes will be parallel to the line of flight. Actually, the square stance advocated here is a slightly opened variation of the perfectly square stance in that, for reasons of balance and power, your lead foot should be turned out toward the target by some 20 to 25 degrees.

As you address the ball, place your right foot—the back foot—on a line dead square to the line of flight; the toe should rest on a line parallel to the line of flight. At first, this will feel unnatural. But don't open your right foot; if you turn the toe to the right, you will ultimately lose control of your body weight during the swing and thus lose power. Plant the toe of your slightly-open right foot against a line parallel to the line of flight—and keep it there. In time, your foot will even feel comfortable in that position.

Now, set your left foot squarely against the line of flight, then simply turn out the toe by some 20 to 25 degrees. As you do this, be careful that you don't move the entire foot behind an imaginary line drawn through the toe of your back foot and parallel to the line of flight. By opening the toe of your left foot in this manner, you will maintain solid balance throughout the swing and will establish a firm base from which you will be able to execute a swing with maximum power and feel.

In assuming your stance over the ball, spread your feet apart at a width that roughly approximates the width of your shoulders (mind you, the width between the feet means the width between your heels, not your toes). It is important that your stance be neither too narrow nor too wide. The wider the stance, the more powerless you will be, since a wide stance restricts what should be the normal flow of body movement during the swing. However, a stance that is too narrow restricts power too; it does not provide you with a solid-enough base from which to coil for power. Invariably, the player whose stance is too narrow tends to lose his or her balance during the backswing and ultimately makes a semi-powerless swipe at the ball.

As you address your ball, your body weight should be evenly distributed —50/50—between both feet and centered on the balls of each foot. Too many amateurs, unfortunately, either lean back on their right foot or forward on their left as they address the ball, while others either lean so far forward that it looks as though they will fall face first onto their ball—or lean so far back on their heels that it looks as if they will fall flat on their rear the instant they take the club back.

This is mainly a matter of mental comfort. Once you have assumed your stance, settle into it naturally, and relax. Too many players take a forced position as they address the ball. The next time you stand over the ball at address, imagine that you are out in the back yard with a spatula in your hand, charcoaling some burgers.

The stance at address. The back foot is square to the line of flight, the left foot is turned out slightly, the ball is off the left heel, the hands are forward, the head is cocked slightly. The body weight should be evenly distributed between both feet.

POSTURE AT ADDRESS

In the long and storied history of the game, no golfer has ever been bitten by a ball. So why is it that so many players look scared stiff as they stand over the ball at address? Or as one player so aptly said, "When I address the ball, I'm about as relaxed as I am when I'm asking my boss for a raise." But there is no reason why you ever should wrap yourself up like a pretzel as you address the ball. It is impossible to play golf—or, for that matter, any other sport—if you approach the swing in a tense, rigid manner. If you are tight and taut at address, you will force the swing—and not permit yourself to move naturally and fluidly.

Let's do it step by step.

You have selected your club and have studied the shot you must play from a position behind the ball that allows you to acquire a definite feel for the shot, one that provides an outline of the flight you want the ball to take. Now, walk

There should be nothing forced or unnatural about your position at address. The picture at the far left illustrates the correct posture at address, with everything in perfect sync. The three illustrations to the right slightly exaggerate the many flaws found at address.

up to the ball and stand beside it. Be loose. Set the club head on the ground behind the ball and assume a comfortable position. As you address the ball, your left arm should not be flexed or rigid; it should be extended in a natural way. Your right arm should drop naturally from the shoulder—don't move it forward or around. The club should feel, and almost look, as though it is a natural extension of your arms. Because the ball is positioned forward in your stance, off the left heel (see following section), it is only natural that your back shoulder will be slightly lower than the front shoulder at address. Think of it this way: a line drawn across the tops of your shoulders should not be parallel to the ground.

The position of the club determines how far away from the ball you stand. As you set up, you must be in a position that allows you to take a natural swing at the ball. You don't want to be too close to the ball—or too far away. There is no set inch-or-foot rule that applies here; simply establish a position in relation to the ball that guarantees you freedom of movement and total comfort. For instance, if you stand too far away from the ball, you will have to lean over and forward in order to make contact; the results, naturally, will be disastrous. If you stand too close to the ball, you will constrict your swing and tend to lift up as you approach impact.

Now, as you line up, set your shoulders and your hips on a line parallel to the target line; they should be parallel to the intended line of flight. The natural tendency is to force your shoulders and your hips open at address, so that they seem to face the target. Don't do this. If you do, you will invariably hit an uncontrolled slice.

The right way to address the ball: hands forward, feet spread comfortably apart, ball off the left heel, weight evenly distributed. On facing page an unnatural address (left), with the hands back off the right leg and the ball back in the stance; and an exaggerated address (right), with the ball far too forward while everything else is well back.

At address, your back should be relatively straight, not hunched. A common flaw of most semi-skilled golfers, as well as some highly skilled shot makers, is that they get to the ball at address—that is, they get their hands into the proper address position—by bending way over from the waist or by bending their knees too much. Such positions will create balance and power problems throughout the swing. To get to the ball, bend your knees slightly; this movement will automatically lower you into the desired position.

Tom Watson, among other good players, seems to stick his butt out as he settles into the address position; in fact, as he addresses the ball, Watson almost looks as though he is about to settle into a chair. There is nothing wrong with this move; Watson is establishing an even more solid base from which to

Jack Nicklaus digs deep to hit this shot, but notice that his head position still has not changed even though the ball already is en route to the target.

execute his swing, and he clears out his middle in such a way that he will not be restricted at all during the swing.

Lastly, as you stand over the ball, relax. Do not—repeat not—be tense or rigid. Be comfortable. Be natural. Be yourself.

POSITION OF THE BALL AT ADDRESS

The old school of golf taught that the position of the ball at address should graduate slightly from the big toe of the left foot to the middle of the right foot as the player moved through the bag of golf clubs, starting with the driver and concluding with the sand wedge. In other words, set the ball off the big toe of

the left foot when using a driver, set it in about the mid
using a five-iron, and set it off the middle of the right f
wedge.

However, the trouble with that theory is this: By
different positions, you introduce a new element to e
different apex of the shot for each club that you swing. Tl
ency.

To latter-day golf instructors, this inconsistency w
time a whole new theory of ball position evolved, one th
Rather than move the ball throughout the stance at addr
a single set position for it? Why not eliminate the inconsistency by eliminating
the variable? Or, to put it another way, why not establish consistency by
establishing a constant? After all, by establishing one ball position for all
full-swing shots, you also create one apex for all your shots.

At address, your dominant, "master" eye (which varies for each individual)
should be in solid contact with the ball. Here, the golfer's master eye is his
left, which is trained on the ball.

or that apex, one trouble area for weekend players is the fact that when ...ish their downswing and reach the point of impact, the ball is not there. ...ybe it was there two or three inches ago. Maybe it will be there in another ...wo or three inches. Whatever, at the apex—that exact point in the swing where the downswing ends at the instant of impact, and where the club head is dead on the target—the ball is not there. The result: a mis-hit shot.

Where should this apex be? A great majority of the best golfers in the world have concluded, after thousands and thousands of test shots on practice ranges, that the apex of the swing should be at a position opposite the left heel as the golfer is set up in the address position. In other words, they have found that the club head will hit the ball at the correct instant if they position the ball off their left heel. When the ball is off their left heel, they have discovered that they are firmer at the apex and, as a result, hit the ball with maximum power, feel, and balance.

The left heel, then, is the optimum location for the position of the ball at address.

Two views of the takeaway. Notice that in both pictures there is a good extension during the first few feet of the backswing and no breaking of the wrists. Notice, too, that there has been no movement of the head.

HEAD POSITION

How many times has your local pro told you, "Keep your head still"? You cannot possibly expect to make solid contact with the golf ball if you move your head—up or down, in or out—during the swing. The head is the axis, the fulcrum, of the swing. If the head moves, everything else automatically moves. And once things start to move during the swing, the ball will move too—in some direction other than the intended one.

One of Jack Nicklaus's favorite stories about golf instruction is how Jack Grout, his teacher, got him, as a teenager, to keep his head absolutely still throughout the swing. Grout would simply station an assistant in front of Nicklaus. As young Jack set up at address, the aide would grab a lock of Nicklaus's hair. If Nicklaus moved his head during the swing—well, it only hurt for a little while.

So, keep your head still—not rigid, but still.

The position of the head should be behind the ball at address, slightly

Ben Crenshaw demonstrates perfect upper body position at the top of his swing: left arm locked, right elbow pointing to the ground, shoulders rotated 90 degrees, and hands high.

cocked to one side or the other. Under no condition should your head ever be ahead of the ball at address; if this happens, your weight will be too far forward and the end result will probably be a shot resembling a shank. In order to maximize your power and achieve full body thrust at impact, your head must remain behind the ball.

The Master Eye

Most professionals cock their head at address too, depending upon which eye is the "master eye" as they sight the ball at address. Everyone has a so-called master, or dominant, eye, and as a general rule, the master eye should determine the way you look at the ball at address. If your master eye is your left eye, you might want to cock your head slightly to the right in order to allow your left eye to sight the ball cleanly and clearly. If your master eye is the right eye, you might want to cock your head slightly to the left so that the right eye can have a better look at the ball.

Finally, in setting your head at address, don't strain it into some uncomfortable position. Some amateur golfers tend to force their head downward so that the chin practically rests against the neck; others raise the head so high that their eyes seem to be looking straight into outer space, not at the ball. Just assume a natural and comfortable head position—behind the ball!

BACKSWING

Now, at long last, you are ready to swing.

The Forward Press

The first movement of the swing is the forward press. Stated simply, the forward press is a movement that concludes the complicated routine of the setup and initiates the actual rhythm of the swing. The forward press launches the swing in motion.

For Gary Player, the forward press is a slight inward turn of his right knee, which signifies that he is satisfied with his setup and is now ready to begin his swing. Other top-rank touring professionals forward-press by working their shoulders forward, while still other pros forward-press by waggling their bodies or their club heads into a pronounced position from which they can launch their attack on the ball.

For the most part, these forward presses require a delicate balance that can be acquired only through constant play. But since even the best amateur golfers can't play every day, the best press for them seems to be the most simple one to execute: the forward press with the hands. Such a press, in fact, serves two purposes.

When most amateurs line up at address and put the club down behind the ball, their hands tend to be right over the ball—or maybe even behind it. Rarely, if ever, will an amateur address the ball with hands in front of the ball. Then, when they start their swing, they move their hands toward the back—the way they should. As a result, the club head trails the hands. By doing this, they eventually create a whipping action with the club head that almost always results in a mis-hit shot. Indeed, if you whip the club head uncontrollably at the start of the swing, you ultimately will sling it or cast it at the top of the backswing in a futile effort to recreate the feeling and rhythm lost at the outset.

On the other hand, by pressing your hands slightly forward—one or two inches—the instant before you begin your takeaway, you not only unitize the feeling between hands and club head, you also get your hands properly in position in front of the ball. And by doing this, you help eliminate the possibility of creating whippiness during the backswing.

Think of it this way. Before you start back, you must go forward—however slightly—with your hands.

A forward press also serves as a strong psychological instrument. People tend to be creatures of habit. You get out of bed on the left side, not the right. You put on your pants before—or after—your shirt. You read the paper after dinner, not before. Whatever. In golf, by establishing a standard forward press before each shot, you develop a definite habit to your golf—one that can only make your game better.

The Takeaway

Now we are into the action part of the swing. Having initiated the swing with a forward press, it is time for the takeaway—or the backswing. Not surprisingly, there are dozens of schools of thought as to how the club should be taken away from the ball. The first move back is most critical. Some teaching professionals think you should start the club back with a move by your left shoulder. Other teaching professionals suggest that the first move back be with your left knee. And in recent years George Fazio, a strong player of the 1940s and 1950s who is now one of the most prominent—and controversial—golf course architects in the world, has convinced a number of top-rank touring professionals that they should launch their backswing by turning their hips to the right before doing anything else. For sure, there are merits to all these suggestions. However, to execute such complicated moves, one must play golf on a regular basis —certainly more frequently than amateur players who strike the ball two days a week at most.

Indeed, for the amateur golfer, the best and simplest way to launch the takeaway is with the left arm and the left hand working in unison. Once they start the club back, everything else will follow in a natural progression. By starting the club back this way, you will have a chance to execute a fairly uncomplicated one-piece swing that is easy to repeat for every shot. On the other hand, a swing that starts with, say, a hip turn is a multi-piece swing and tends to become endlessly complicated.

As you bring the club back, it is imperative that you maintain a fluid rhythm. Don't lift the club with a pronounced jerk as you take it back. Swing it back on a naturally extended plane at a speed you can maintain without extra effort. It is impossible to control a slow, labored backswing, just as it is impossible to control a fast, whippy backswing. There is a happy medium somewhere between a fast takeaway and a slow takeaway, and the place where you will find that happy medium is on the practice tee. Through constant repetition you will develop a backswing speed that you can handle. As a general rule, the slower the backswing the better; there are few, if any, players of quality who have used what you might call a fast backswing. A backswing, though, must not be *too* slow, or it will lead to a dreaded pickup of the club during the takeaway and, ultimately, a bad shot.

Once you start to take the club back, the easiest way out is to bring it back to the inside—almost to the point that you rub your hands against your right side. Too many amateurs unfortunately tend to do just that, and it ultimately causes them countless problems—mainly in the area of the shoulders, which must then rotate quickly and unnaturally at the top of the backswing in order to get the club onto the proper swing plane. Forget that.

In taking the club back, try to have it describe a plane that is as perfectly straight along the line of flight as possible. Of course, as the club head begins to disappear from your peripheral vision, it will naturally move to the inside, away from the line of flight. But if you can keep the club head moving straight back—not outside, not inside—for as long as you can see it, you are on the way to hitting a solid shot. Very few players can take the club back inside and make good contact, but many players—particularly powerful hitters—can take the club back on a line that is slightly outside and then make a good solid hit. Why? Because of their power, and because they have perfected such a move through constant practice.

To the Top

All right. You are taking the club head back on a plane that describes the line of flight, and you are taking it back at a fairly slow and rhythmic speed.

In moving back, your hands must not get out of sync with your shoulders, and your left arm must remain as straight as possible, with no pronounced break or hinging at the elbow. Don't let your hands snap the club head back too quickly; they must work as a unit, not as independent parts. Some amateurs tend to accelerate the cocking of their wrists, doing the cocking as soon as they launch their takeaway and completing it by the time their hands pass their right side. This is wrong. The wrists should not even begin to cock until they have passed the hips during the takeaway. And then the cocking is done gradually, not in any forced way.

Once the left arm and the left hand together begin to take the club back, the left shoulder, the left hip, and the left foot also begin to get involved in the swing in a highly natural way. Of course, at the same time, when the left shoulder becomes active, it also activates the right shoulder, and when the left hip is in motion, the right hip also becomes active; considering the scope of the movement you are trying to execute, it is impossible to isolate the action of either one of the hips or either one of the shoulders. At the top of the backswing, the shoulders will have revolved approximately twice as much as the hips; the shoulders turning almost 90 degrees, the hips about 45 degrees.

As for the legs, they are a different matter.

On the backswing, you must not let your body weight pass to the outside of your right foot; in effect, you should use the inside of your right foot and also your slightly turned-in right knee as braces to work against during the takeaway. If either the right foot or the right knee sway to the outside, you will immediately fall off balance and put yourself into a lunging position.

At the top of the backswing, your left shoulder should be slightly under your chin, positioned in such a way that it does not impair your look at the ball; if the left shoulder is well to the left of the chin at the top of the backswing, you have not completed it and are not in a solid position to execute the rest of the swing.

Your right elbow should be pointing to the ground, not into outer space to create what golf instructors like to call the "flying elbow." In bringing the club back, your right elbow should cling as closely to your side as is naturally possible.

Your left knee should be pointed to the right of the ball, not at the ball or to the left of it. If your left knee does not point to the right of the ball, you have not executed a good takeaway because you have shortened it in some way. However, you should not be thinking about the direction of your left knee as you bring the club back; the left knee should automatically move into the proper position.

Don't worry whether your left heel is on or off the ground. Whatever happens, let it happen. If you consciously try to keep your heel on the ground or off the ground, you will destroy the natural rhythm of the takeaway. Some golfers are constructed in such a way that they do not naturally lift their left heel during the takeaway—and there is no reason why they should force themselves to do it.

At the top, your body should be balanced with 70 percent of your weight on the right side and 30 percent on the left; this weight shift should be a natural transition, not a forced move.

Meanwhile, at the peak of the backswing, the shaft of the club should be on a line that is parallel—not past parallel or pre-parallel—to the target line. And your hands should be held high, as high as humanly possible. It is important, too, that there be no breakage in the area of the left wrist at the top of the backswing, or else you will cast the club at the start of the downswing and hit a big slice.

Pause at the Top

The pause at the top is not golf's equivalent of a coffee break. Don't drop everything and take a breather. Put simply, the pause at the top is that exact split second where the backswing terminates and the downswing begins. It may well be an optical illusion, but for one fleeting instant it seems as though everything has stopped. Actually, your hips are turning.

Whatever you do, do not consciously pause at the top of your backswing —or else you will destroy the natural rhythm and feeling that you worked so hard to create during the takeaway. And once that happens, you will lose control of the club and make a powerless swipe at the ball. Understand that there is a pause, but don't worry about it.

The swing in sequence. It starts with a sound fundamental position at address, ball off the left heel, weight evenly distributed, head cocked slightly, hands forward, left foot turned slightly out, knees flexed, stance square. As the hands lead the club through the takeaway, there is no wrist break until after the hands pass the right side. Approaching the top, the arms and the club are fully extended, the left knee is pointed at the ball, and the hips are rotating. Still approaching the top, the left heel is now off the

ground and the left knee is aimed squarely at the ball. At the top of the backswing, there is an imaginary pause as one part of the swing concludes and another begins. Note that the club never passes a point that is parallel to the ground. Note, too, that the position of the head has not changed during the backswing and that the left arm has remained solid, with no break at the elbow. Everything is moving forward now, the left heel having returned to the ground, and the club is uncoiling.

Approaching impact, everything is still going forward in a powerful motion, but the head position has not changed. At impact, the hips are opening and the legs are driving forward, but the head remains locked in a solid position. After impact, the club continues through the shot and the right foot begins to come off the ground, but still the head has not moved. Note the excellent extension of the club as it works through to a high finish. Everything remains in proper balance.

Starting the Downswing

Because most athletes like to "hit" something, golfers tend to launch their downswing with some movement of the hands and shoulders. This is a common fault, but one that can—and must—be corrected. If the hands initiate the downswing, you will cast the club, almost as if you are casting a fishing rod, and toss it off the intended plane to the ball. Casting leads to puff balls or duck hooks or groaning slices. Once you cast the club, your whole swing is suddenly out of sync and it becomes impossible to correct the pattern of your swing in the fraction of a second it takes you to move from the top of the backswing to the point of impact.

On the whole, the downswing itself hardly requires the demanding technical precision of the takeaway. The reason for this is that the downswing is conducted at a far greater speed.

Start the downswing not by flailing away with your hands but, instead, by turning your lower body in a precise pattern. At the top, your hands remain momentarily in place—thus creating the illusion of a pause at the top—as you make the first move down with your hips. Your hips, which had rotated some 45 degrees to the back during the backswing, begin to rotate forward, and your body weight naturally begins to shift forward. Simultaneously, your left heel, which probably came off the ground during the takeaway, also begins to return to the ground. And then, suddenly, with everything moving forward, the hands follow in turn—bringing the club down to the ball. Everything should be in perfect sync.

Club-head Speed

If you have ever watched a professional golf tournament, you have probably wondered—even aloud—how a player the size of, say, Chi Chi Rodriguez, who is all of five feet seven inches and 130 pounds, can drive the ball as long as someone who stands six foot four and weighs 230 pounds. The answer is that Rodriguez, by making strong and sharp moves throughout his swing, generates so much club-head speed at impact that he can rocket the ball the prodigious distances reached by big strong players, who perhaps depend more on their physical prowess for distance.

Nancy Lopez unleashes mightily into the ball (left), then stays down on the shot with a full extension of the club (right).

At Impact

As you make precise contact with the ball, everything, of course, is still moving forward. At impact, your left shoulder should be moving up and around, while your right shoulder should be moving down and around. At the same time, your left ankle should be rolling to the outside as the weight begins to move to the outside. At impact, however, most of your weight should be set on the inside of your left foot. As you make contact with the ball, there must be a firmness to your left side; in fact, you should have the feeling that you are "hitting" against your left side as you make contact.

Following Through

Once you have made contact with the ball, keep going. Complete your swing by making a good follow-through, letting your body motion run its course. After impact, keep your hips turning until they face dead on at the target. Keep your hands working forward—with a strong, full extension—until there is no farther forward to go, at which time the hands will naturally bring the club head up and back over your left shoulder. On the follow-through, your weight gradually moves left, and at the completion of the swing your weight should be about 90 percent on your left foot—with the other 10 percent perched almost on the toe of your right foot, the heel having left the ground.

In short, force yourself to make a good follow-through, a natural follow-through. Don't quit on the shot after impact.

Don't ever quit on a shot after impact; the ball will not take full flight. Extend your swing to a natural follow-through.

Putting

In 1976, Joseph C. Dey, Jr., longtime executive director of the United States Golf Association and later commissioner of the PGA tour, was appointed Captain of the Royal and Ancient Golf Club of St. Andrews, Scotland, and spent most of that year living there. One day, Mr. Dey came across this verse composed by an ancient Scot named W. M. Lindsay:

> Of all the strokes that's in the game,
> Which is your choice? Give it a name.
> The drive, say you; the loft, say you;
> The brassie shot, the cleek shot—
> But give me the putt.
> The wee bit pat, no more than that;
> The canny touch, scarcely so much.
> The stroke that sends the ballie in,
> O that's the stroke to make you win!

When a professional on the PGA tour, hardly a playground for poets, read Mr. Lindsay's verse, he said, "It's just like we all say out here on the tour: Drive for show and putt for dough."

Not very eloquent, perhaps, but true.

Golf basically is designed as a par-72 game, with a round of perfect par golf consisting of an equal number of shots and putts, 36 of each. Few

93

For and all golfers, putting is the name of the game.

players ever achieve that delicate balance during a round, however, even on the pro tours. "It's easier to play sub-par golf on the greens than it is on the rest of the course," says one pro. "When I shoot a 72, I usually hit somewhere between 39 and 43 shots and take somewhere between 29 and 33 putts. But I've had rounds of 72 where I've had 47 shots and 25 putts, and I've had rounds of 72 where I've had 32 shots and 40 putts. What I'd really like to have, just once, is a round with 32 shots and 25 putts."

Putting is golf's great equalizer. It is the most individual aspect of the game, and the one area—the only area—where you can do your own thing and expect to have success. In putting, the weak can get even with the strong and the worst 32-handicap hacker can work as effectively as the U.S. Open champion. To strike a golf shot, you must execute a number of different and often complicated fundamentals; the golf swing is highly complex. In putting, though, there are few fundamentals—and fewer complications. The putting stroke is an extremely short movement, so the player does not need a big swing

Putters come in all sizes and shapes. Find one that works for you and stick with it.

and a lot of muscle in order to score well on the greens. To putt well, to putt consistently, all you really need is touch, feel, and good hand-eye coordination.

SELECTING A PUTTER

Putters come in all sizes and shapes. There are putters that look like hot dogs, putters that look like bottles, even some that look like doughnuts with a bite taken on one side. And putters tend to have strange-sounding names—"Zebra," "Bull's-Eye," "Ping," "Potato Masher," "Cash-In," and "La Femme." Don't laugh. Those exotically named putting devices have been used by some of the greatest names in golf's history. In 1967, Jack Nicklaus won the U.S. Open at Baltusrol by using a putter he had named "White Fang"; actually, it was a brass bull's-eye putter that Nicklaus's wife, Barbara, painted white each night.

Four favorite putters (from left): the flange blade, the mallet, the center-shafted bull's eye, and one of the many models of the ever-popular Ping.

Kinds of Putters

Basically, all putters are either center shafted or blade, with several hundred available variations of each. A center-shafted putter is one where the blade extends in both directions from the shaft; a blade putter is one where the shaft is at one end and the blade extends from that shaft. For the most part, these hundreds of variations also tend to fall into one of three categories: straight blade, flange blade, or mallet head. The straight-blade putter head is just that: a thinly bladed head that is most suited for putting on ultra-fast, ultra-slick greens. The flange blade is a straight blade with a flangelike extension protruding from the lower part of the back side of the head. The mallet head is a heavy-headed putter that is shaped like a half moon.

In recent years the manufacturers of putters have worked overtime to create a putter head with what might be called total life. In other words, they have tried to make the entire face of the head into one big "sweet spot." With many of these total-life putters, a player will get the same roll and distance from a putt stubbed on the toe or the heel as from a putt hit squarely in the center of the blade. Also, with these putters the ball tends to "pop" off the face. However, many of golf's best players prefer to use putters that have one definite sweet spot, preferably in the middle of the blade; they like to use the deader parts of the putter blade for controlling the shorter, more delicate "speed" putts they face each round. For example, many good putters like to play their short, twisting, downhill putts by striking the ball out on the toe of the putter face. By doing this, they deaden the putt and can more easily control the roll of the ball.

The basic rules for selecting a putter are these:

1. If the greens on which you play most of your rounds of golf are *always* fast and slick, you should use a light blade putter that provides maximum feel and touch.

2. If the greens are sometimes fast and sometimes slow, you should use a flange-blade putter that will provide a sense both of good feel and of good hit.

3. If the greens you usually play are almost always slow and bumpy, you might want to try a mallet-head putter because it will provide the maximum possible hit without requiring an abnormally muscular putting rhythm.

Popularity of the Flange Blade

The putter used by most players on both tours is the flange blade. Jack Nicklaus, Lee Trevino, and Arnold Palmer have used flange blades for almost their entire professional careers; Nicklaus, in fact, has used the same flange blade for all but about fifteen tournaments since he turned professional in 1961, while Palmer has used perhaps 150 different flange-blade-style putters since he turned professional in the mid-1950s. But there are great players who don't use the flange blade: Billy Casper, for instance, has always putted with a mallet head; Hubert Green has a pure blade putter that was made sometime during the early 1920s; and Tom Watson generally uses a center-shafted, total-life putter with a slight flange protrusion.

The major reason for the popularity of the flange blade among golf's better players is that it is the happy medium between the pure blade and the mallet head and thus the right putter for all courses. Unlike most golfers, who play the same course perhaps 95 percent of the time they tee up, touring pros and those amateurs who take their competition seriously invariably play greens of different texture and quality as they move around from tournament to tournament each week. One week they may play slow Bermuda-grass greens in the desert, the next week, fast bent-grass greens in Ohio. Rather than switch putters each time and try to become accustomed to a new feel, they settle on the one putter with which they can survive on all kinds of greens.

So if you play a lot of tournament golf, or play on a lot of different courses, the flange blade is the right putter for you. If you don't play a lot of tournament golf, or on a lot of different courses, follow the basic rules given for selecting a putter.

Whatever you do, though, don't become a chronic putter switcher. Find one putter and stick with it. After all, the putter does not miss the putt; you do.

Marker

The putter you use should have a marker of some sort on the top of the head, right at the edge leading to the position of the ball as you address the putt. This marker will help you line up your ball along its intended path, and also enable you to start the ball along the intended line by having the putter head strike the ball squarely at the point where the marker meets the ball. If you use a putter without a marker, you may have no sense of direction as you stand over the ball and get ready to putt.

Lie

Once you select a putter that looks good and feels good, make certain that—like all your other clubs—it rests in its natural-soled position when you stand over the ball in your preferred address position. If the putter head rests on either its toe or its heel, thus causing a part of the head to be off the ground at address, you may stub the head sometime before impact and, as a result, mis-hit your putt. (True, Isao Aoki, the brilliant Japanese golfer, putts with the toe of his putter well off the ground and is, as he proved during his classic confrontations with Nicklaus in the 1980 U.S. Open, a great putter. But the Aokis are a rarity.)

Angle and Length

Since putting is the most individual thing in golf, players can use putting stances that happen to suit their own tastes. But if you use a hands-high, stand-up putting stroke, be certain that you also use a very upright putter; if you like to bend over and hold your hands low, down almost on your knees—the way Hubert Green does—you should select a putter that fits such a stance. The length of the putter shaft, too, is a matter of individual taste. Try various lengths, then decide for yourself what length provides you with the best touch and feel—and the most comfort.

THE GRIP

Because putting is essentially a right-handed game, meaning that the right hand is the dominant hand during the stroke, it is imperative that the player have as much right-hand control over the putter as possible. For this reason, there is a special grip used just for putting: the "reverse overlap." Remember the basic overlapping grip discussed in chapter 3, where four fingers of your left hand and three fingers of your right hand rest on the shaft of the club? Well, with the reverse overlap grip for putting, three fingers of the left hand and four of the right hand rest on the grip. By getting all four fingers of your right hand, as well as the thumb of the right hand, firmly on the shaft, the player is assured of having maximum control over the movement of the putter.

To assume a reverse overlap grip, simply take the four fingers of your right hand and wrap them comfortably around the shaft of the club, then wrap your left hand around the shaft so that the left index finger overlaps between the last two fingers of your right hand. Both thumbs should be set squarely down the center of the shaft.

Gripping the putter. First, the thumb of the left hand should be set squarely up and down the flat front of the grip (left). Then the right thumb adopts the same position lower on the shaft (right), with the palm aiming square at the target.

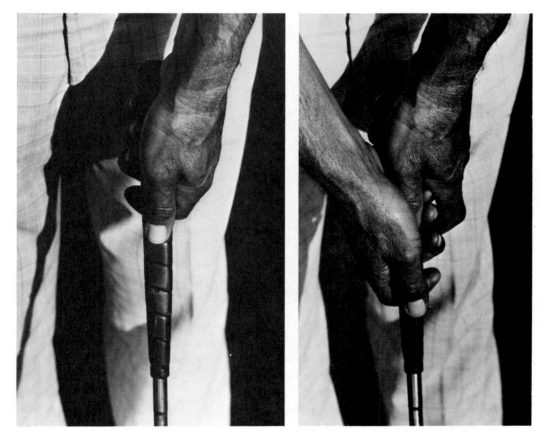

Choose a putter that has a grip with a flat surface on the front; such a grip makes it easy to keep your thumbs set squarely down the center of the shaft. There are various models of putter grips, too, ranging from pistol-style to paddle-style. When selecting a putter, make certain that it has a grip which is so comfortable that it practically feels as though it is part of your hands.

As you address a putt, the palm of the right hand should be aligned squarely at your target—that is, along the line on which you want to start your putt rolling. The back of the left hand should be set slightly, and quite naturally, to the left of your intended line.

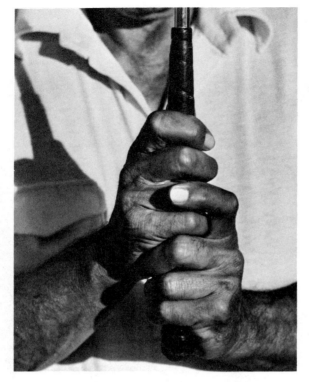

The reverse overlap grip is the correct grip for putting because it puts all four fingers of the right hand on the club, all the better for a stroke that is predominantly right-handed.

In the putting grip, the key pressure points are the left thumb, which must rest tightly against the shaft, and the index finger and thumb of the right hand, both of which provide much of the feel behind the stroke. Don't strangle the putter as you hold it in your hands, and don't hold it too tenderly either. The trick is to find the right touch by establishing a unitized working relationship between your hands and the putter, something that can be acquired only through regular practice on the putting green or the living room rug.

THE SETUP

If you closely inspect the actions of, say, Tom Watson, Ben Crenshaw, or Nancy Lopez-Melton as they stand over a putt, you will immediately detect that they rarely, if ever, stand over any two putts the same way. Watch. They may widen their stance a millimeter for one putt, then narrow it for the next. Or they may open their stance slightly for one putt, then square it for the next. Or they may cock their head back and drop it slightly for one putt, then raise the head and set it directly over the ball for the next. They may crouch for one

When putting, your eyes should be directly over the ball so that they see the same roll that the ball sees. And be sure the hands are slightly ahead of the ball at address.

putt, slouch for the next, then stand fairly upright for a third. Indeed, it is not unusual for a top player to use as many as a dozen different putting setups during one 18-hole round.

Why? Comfort. You simply cannot handle the delicate matter of putting unless you feel totally comfortable as you address the ball. And what feels comfortable on, say, the third green may not feel so comfortable on the fourth. But don't be alarmed. If the best golfers in the world cannot set up in the same way for every single putt, why should you?

However, while top golfers may well appear to alter their setups from putt to putt in order to acquire that certain feel that is so necessary in putting, they nevertheless always retain the essentials of the setup in some form or another. For instance, while the position of the head may change slightly from one putt to another, the head itself *always* remains in such a position that the player's eyes are over the golf ball—perhaps directly over the ball or maybe behind it.

The positions of body, ball, head, hands, and elbows form the essentials of the setup.

Body Position

Don't really worry about your stance. Find a comfortable position and settle into it. However, try to be either square to the target—with both feet on a line parallel to the ball—or slightly open, with the lead foot set slightly back from the right. Both these stances offer the best possible look at the target line. In putting, you must also operate from a solid base, so set your feet comfortably apart. The closer your feet, the greater the chance that unwanted body movement will creep into your putting stroke, particularly on longer putts.

Ball Position

Establish a consistent position for the ball as you address your putt; it is impossible to putt successfully if you line up the ball opposite, say, your right foot for one putt and then opposite your left foot for the next. By establishing a single position, you not only eliminate a variable—one that cannot help your putting stroke—but also the element of indecision. When you stand over a putt, you must feel secure; indecision translates to three putts instead of one.

As for the position of the ball, the great majority of so-called super putters play the ball off their left heel, a natural position that requires no physical strain to maintain—and offers maximum comfort.

Head Position

Your head should be directly over the golf ball; in fact, as you stand over a putt, your eyes and the golf ball should be in such a position that they represent the ends of an imaginary straight line. Some golfers vary this position slightly by cocking their head and thus setting it in a position that is behind the ball. In doing this, though, they still make certain that their head remains *over* the ball. Indeed, it is absolutely imperative that the eyes of the golfer always remain in perfect alignment with the golf ball. In other words, the eyes of the golfer and the ball itself both must "see" the same line. If you line up in such a way that your eyes are not in this perfect alignment, you will see a line that the ball does not, and as a result you will not stroke the putt along its intended line. And once you position your head directly over the ball, keep it perfectly still throughout the putting stroke. If you move your head during the stroke, you will unintentionally move the putter head away from its intended path and, of course, eventually mis-hit the putt and miss the hole.

Position of the Hands

In putting, the hands must be set slightly ahead of the ball at address. Do not exaggerate this position. By getting your hands only slightly forward, you set them in a natural position from which you can hit the putt firmly, not sloppily. The putting stroke must be a rhythmic motion, one without any jerkiness, and by setting your hands slightly forward, you are in a position to achieve maximum control. On the other hand, if you set your hands behind the ball as you address the putt, you will have to pick up the putter on the way back in order to keep it from digging into the turf. Such a movement will only destroy the natural rhythm so necessary in the putting stroke. To determine what is the proper forward position for your hands, simply go to the putting green—or even the living room rug—and stroke several putts, altering your hand position for each. You will soon discover that there will be a different feel to each putt; some putts will roll aimlessly while others roll firmly and solidly along the intended line. Because putting is so much a matter of feel and touch, let the feel of the stroke—of the ball reacting off the putter head—determine exactly where you should position your hands ahead of the ball. Ahead. Not behind.

Position of the Elbows

Put simply, the right elbow should remain "in"—that is, pointed to your body —and the left elbow should remain "out" during the putting stroke. To point the right elbow "out" would be very unnatural and would restrict the putting stroke. By keeping the left "out" you will be able to make a proper and natural follow-through to your putting stroke.

THE STROKE

To quote an old philosopher, nothing rolls like a ball. The trick in putting is to get the golf ball rolling. Around and around and around. What you definitely don't want to do is putt the ball in such a way as to cut it, top it, or bang it —that is, make it skid like an uncontrolled knuckleball rather than roll naturally. How do you get that ball to *roll* into the cup? By stroking it.

The arm stroke. As this sequence shows, the left arm guides the club back squarely on line, then the right arm takes over en route through the ball. The

There are basically three types of putting strokes: arm, wrist, and a combination of arm and wrist. Because putting is so much a game of comfort and feel—physically as well as psychologically—even the best golfers in the world tend to alter their putting strokes fairly regularly. Once a top-level professional feels that, say, a stiff-wristed, all-arm putting stroke is not working very well, he or she almost certainly will try some other type of stroke in the next tournament.

The Arm Stroke

In the arm stroke, the arms do almost all the work. The left arm guides the club back on the line, the right arm takes over on the way through the ball—

stiff-wristed right hand supplies the "hit" and keeps the club moving toward the target after impact.

with the stiff-wristed right hand coming into play at impact by supplying much of the touch, feel, and force for the hit—and then keeps the club moving toward the target after impact. Arm putting offers consistency, but at the same time arm putters tend to stroke the ball with less inherent feel because their hands are dormant throughout the greater part of the stroke. One word of caution: In arm putting, never rotate your shoulders and your body in order to get the putter—and your arms—back. Any shoulder movement should follow the natural inclination started by the movement of your arms.

The wrist stroke. The right hand does almost all the work in this putting technique. The right hand brings the putter back, then provides all the touch, feel, and force as the wrists break into the ball at impact, before

The Wrist Stroke

In the wrist stroke, the right hand does almost all the work. The right hand brings the putter back, then provides all the touch, feel, and force as the wrists break into the ball at impact. The left hand plays the guide role throughout the wrist stroke.

leading the putter into the follow-through directly at the target. Notice here how low the putter head remains to the ground throughout the stroke.

The Arm and Wrist Stroke

In the combination arm-wrist stroke, the left arm brings the putter back, then the right hand more or less assumes command by leading the club through the ball and providing the wrist hit as well as the feel and touch at impact.

All things considered, the combination arm and wrist stroke would seem to be the best stroke for those golfers who play mainly on weekends, primarily because it offers the player a better chance to make a consistent hit with plenty of touch and feel.

Basic Stroke Elements

Whatever putting stroke you employ, the fundamental elements of the stroke must never change.

Straight Back, Straight Through

Always—always—take the putter back and then through the ball on a straight line direct for your target, as straight as humanly possible. Don't waver even a fraction of an inch. Mind you, there are some players who maintain that you can putt successfully by moving the blade on an outside-to-inside path and others who insist that you can putt successfully by using an inside-to-outside path. Good luck to them. Such styles require absolute precision; indeed, the putter head—moving out-to-in or in-to-out—must strike the ball at the fleeting instant when the head happens to be passing on a direct line for the target, or else the ball will never take its intended line of roll. It may be easy for a touring pro or a top-level amateur to repeat such an out-to-in or in-to-out putting movement, but the weekend golfer should avoid such a style and stick with the straight-back, straight-through way of putting. It's clearly the safest way to get the ball rolling along the intended path to the cup.

Low club head

Throughout the stroke, you should also keep the putter head as low to the ground as possible. Don't drag it across the grass, but don't pick it up either. By keeping the putter low, you will create a definite consistency in your stroke, because the head of the putter will always be on somewhat the same plane as the golf ball itself. Or, to look at it another way, if you pick up the putter, there is a good chance that instead of stroking the ball at impact and getting it rolling naturally, you will, instead, chop at the ball and send it careening aimlessly.

Steady tempo

In stroking a putt, you also must maintain a consistent tempo. Too many players, unfortunately, either yank the putter back and then whip it through the ball or take the putter back slowly and deliberately and then—almost with a lurch—launch an all-out attack on the ball by taking a hard swipe at it. As you stroke the ball, take the club back on a consistent speed, then try to maintain that same *tempo,* that same speed, as you make contact with the ball and continue into the natural follow-through of the stroke. Many players tend to accelerate the speed of the putter head very slightly as they approach the point of impact. There is nothing wrong with this, as long as it is a gentle acceleration, not a forced swipe. Some players, sad to say, tend to decelerate through the stroke as they approach impact; this is one of the most fatal flaws in putting. The putting stroke should be an easy, relaxed movement, not something that is rushed and forced.

Length

The length of the putting stroke is a highly individualized matter, totally dependent upon the ability of the individual golfer to develop a certain putting rhythm and tempo. In general, the length of the takeaway depends on both the length of the putt and the terrain over which the ball must travel. Say a putt is 20 feet. No golfer can press a button and automatically roll a putt exactly 20 feet. Instead, the golfer must acquire a "feel" for the length of the putt—for the 20 feet—and then adjust the takeaway accordingly to maintain a rhythmic movement throughout the stroke. This feel can be acquired only by constant practice, but once you have acquired it, you should know automatically how long the takeaway should be for each putt. Obviously, the longer the putt, the longer the takeaway—the shorter the putt, the shorter the takeaway.

Contact

Finally, as you stroke a putt, the putter head should make contact with the golf ball while it is slightly on the upswing—not on the downswing or while squarely on the ground. If you hit the ball while the putter is on the downswing or even while it is squarely on the ground, the ball will shoot off, not roll away. Worse still, the ball will bump and bounce and skid and consequently will be totally out of control. By hitting the ball while the putter head is slightly on the upswing, you immediately get the ball rolling over—and under control. So don't skid the ball, roll it.

READING GREENS

Perhaps the No. 1 lament expressed by all golfers is, "Gee, I misread that putt. I thought for sure it was going to break two inches to the left, but it broke three inches to the right. I couldn't believe my eyes." Indeed, reading greens is the toughest part of the game of golf, unless you happen to be a computer in your spare time. One simply does not walk onto a green and immediately calculate the speed, break, and grain involved in a particular putt. It takes time—and practice—to acquire this ability. Even then, putting often becomes as much a matter of luck as skill. Says one PGA tour pro, "Come to think of it, I really don't think I've ever hit a perfect putt."

To stake out a putt, stand halfway between your ball and the cup to get a better feel for the roll and the distance.

Basically, reading a green involves four different elements: the speed of the green, the roll of the putting surface, the grain of the grass on the putting surface, and the length of the putt.

The Speed of the Green

The speed of the green depends mainly on the condition of the grass. One way to help determine this condition is to hit several practice putts on the putting green before you start out on your round. Since the texture of the grass on putting greens is usually the same texture as the grass on the regular greens, you will be able to acquire a feel for the speed of the greens during your practice. Also, always be aware of the height of the grass. If it's high, you probably will have to hit your putts a bit firmer than normal. In assessing the speed of a green, when you line up your putt, remember that the ball will not get to the hole unless you hit it hard enough.

The Roll of the Surface

The roll or contours of a putting surface should be immediately evident to the naked eye, but the subtleties within that roll may well defy even the practiced eye of the surveyor. To determine the general roll your ball will take, study your putt from behind the ball. Consider how many hills, bumps, holes, swales, and other impediments there are between your ball and the cup. Take them in order, assess the results, and then decide how you must play the putt.

One way to double-check the accuracy of your reading is to plumb-bob the surface between your ball and the cup. Engineers use plumb bobs to tell how the land lies, and that is what you want to do. It is a simple operation. Stand or kneel behind the ball and hold the putter at the top of the grip with two fingers of your right hand. Let the club dangle. Now, line the bottom of the shaft of the putter squarely on the ball, so that the ball is behind the shaft. Then look at the top of the shaft—and somewhere up there you will see the flagstick.

If the pin happens to fall on the left side of the shaft, that means the green is slanted or tilted to the left—so you have a right-to-left break on your putt to the hole. If the pin falls on the right side of the shaft, the break is left to right.

Some words of caution. Plumb-bobbing will not tell you how fast the green is, nor will it tell you anything about the texture of the green. Also, since the theory behind the plumb-bob technique is that a hanging object will fall toward the center of the earth, don't expect to plumb-bob successfully if you use a mallet-headed putter, since a mallet is weighted on one side of the head.

Plumb-bobbing a putt requires a
center-shafted putter.

The Grain of the Green

Grain is the direction in which the grass grows and bends, both factors directly affecting the speed and the direction of a putt. Reading grain is tricky. In the simplest terms, if the grass looks light and silvery when you stand at the front of a green, it is growing away from you. But if the grass looks brown and dark, it is growing toward you. Obviously, if you are putting *with* the grain, you do not have to hit the ball as hard as you do if you are putting *into* or *against* the grain. If you happen to have a putt that is across the grain, always allow for a little more—or a little less—break than you read into the putt, depending, of course, on the other factors involved in the original decisions. And a word

of caution: Grain greatly affects the direction of a slowly moving putt. So, on
grainy greens, be particularly firm with your short putts, or else they will roll
away from the cup as the ball loses speed.

The Length of the Putt

Finally, there are ways to determine the approximate length of a putt. Pace off
the distance, particularly for longer putts—anything longer than, say, 20 feet
—by striding toward the hole along a line somewhat the same as the line of your
putt. As a rough approximation, one regular step equals three feet. So if the
distance between your ball and the cup is, say, twelve paces, the distance of the
putt is about 36 feet. Now, a 36-foot putt does not automatically tell you that
your takeaway must be, say, two feet long, but knowing that a putt must travel
36 feet provides reassurance as you prepare to stroke the ball.

THE MENTAL GAME

In one way, putting is much like playing quarterback on a football team; neither
the quarterback nor the putter will succeed without a fundamentally sound and
well-conceived game plan. And just as the quarterback should always be thinking several plays ahead, so should you, the putter.

For instance, the next time you play a round of golf, try plotting your
putting strategy for each hole when you are standing back on the fairway, or
in the rough, and debating what club and what type of shot you must hit to
get the ball onto the putting surface. Indeed, as any pro will tell you, putting
actually begins with the approach shot to the green.

Unless you are a touring professional, you probably play the same golf
course nine rounds out of ten. So you should be quite familiar with the forma-
tion of each and every green on that course. In addition, you also should be
well aware of your particular strengths and weaknesses as a putter. Do you
handle right-to-left breaks better than left-to-right breaks? Do you quiver over
downhill putts but stand tall over uphill putts?

You should always try to leave your approach shot to the green in such
a position that you have—in your own mind, at least—the easiest possible putt
to the hole. Often that easiest putt may be a 20-footer straight uphill rather than
a 4-foot downhill-sidehill slider. To quote one top pro, "I age one week every
time I even think about a downhill putt. And if it's a downhill putt that breaks
left to right, I age two weeks."

Once you hit your approach shot and start walking to the green, try to block everything out of your mind except the putt you soon will be facing. Try to recall what happened the last time you putted on the same green. What did the ball do? How did it break? Try to acquire a familiarity with the green. And as you get closer to it, give your putt a long-range read. Check where the ball

rests in relation to the pin. Say that the ball is on the right side of the green
as you approach the putting surface. Is the pin uphill or downhill from the ball?
How does the green slant? Right? Left? Front? Back? By giving the green a
pre-read of sorts, you will acquire a good feel for it and then be able to line up
your putts with even more confidence.

When it comes to putting, practice
makes perfect. Putting to a target is
imperative.

Once you are on the green, don't start to engage in small talk with your playing companions, and don't stand idly off to the side admiring the shrubbery. Work on your putt! Study your line while the other players in your group are putting. If a playing companion happens to make a putt that covers much the same line that you expect your putt to travel, study its roll and learn from it. And if you are playing early in the morning on greens that are still wet, look for some ball markings made by previous players that might serve as a guide for your putt. By doing all these things, you keep yourself in the game—and make putting an easier business.

All smart golfers also make one important decision as they line up a putt: whether they will try to make the putt or be happy to two-putt the green. On the whole, the name of the game is two-putting. Eliminate the three-putt greens, and you will be ahead of the game. Why do people three-putt a green? Probably because they tried to hole a putt from some great distance.

However, you should try to make all the 3-, 5-, 10-, and 20-footers you face each round, since most golfers normally do not three-putt with great regularity from those relatively short distances. But once a putt is longer than approximately 20 feet, a decision must be made: Do you want to go for that putt and, if you miss it, risk three-putting, or do you want to get safely down into the cup in two easy putts?

Most touring pros handle these longer putts in one of two ways, depending on the slope of the putting surface around the cup.

1. If the area around the cup is relatively flat, or at least flat enough that a short putt will not have a sharp, severe break, the pros outline a circle around the cup, perhaps two feet in diameter, with the hole as the center, and then try to get their putt to stop somewhere within that circle. Maybe their putt will drop into the cup, maybe not. But if it doesn't fall, and long putts are hardly automatic, they will be left with a relatively short, straight putt of no longer than two feet.

2. If the area around the cup is sharply contoured on one or two or even three sides, the pros will mentally block out those areas and try to putt into the area around the cup that offers the easiest possible second putt. On some occasions, they will not even risk running the ball at the cup, in the event that they might roll it past and into a position from which the next putt will be even more difficult.

Now, don't think that these attitudes toward long putts represent negative thinking. In fact, you're thinking positively, not negatively, when you rule out the idea of sinking a particular long putt since, as they say, the best long putt is usually a *good* miss.

PRACTICE

Putting is work, so work at it, not only on the putting green but even on the rugs at home. The more you putt, the more you will develop a feel—for your putter, for the golf ball, and for the target. Once you coordinate a definite feel for all these elements, you will have gained much of the confidence that you need to putt well and consistently.

When you practice your putting, always putt to a target. Don't just putt idly at nothing. On a putting green, this means you should putt at a cup—or perhaps a ball or a club head or club cover placed on the green. On the rug at home, use a glass, a napkin, an ashtray, anything.

While you should work at putting, be careful that you don't overdo it. For instance, if you are having trouble finding a workable stroke or getting comfortable over the ball, go to the practice green, drop a few balls, and then try to find what you might call a working groove. Once you acquire this groove—and it might require anywhere from one to even a hundred putts—don't belabor the issue. Instead, when you feel comfortable, when you feel you have rediscovered your putting stroke, pick up your golf balls and your putter and go home. By staying on the practice green too long, you risk the possibility of losing that comfort and feel.

The Circle Drill

The best type of formal practice putting is something called the circle drill. To do this exercise, simply line up a number of golf balls in a circle around the hole, as close to or as far away from the cup as you wish. By placing these balls in positions around the cup, rather than placing them in one basic spot, you will be faced with a slightly different putt each time. One putt may break left to right; the next may be straight; the one after that may break right to left; and the fourth putt may go downhill and break to the right. Whatever, the circle drill offers variety and eliminates the monotony from practice putting.

ting Checkpoints

Find one putter—and stick with it.
· Use the reverse overlap grip.
· Don't strangle the club.
· Find a comfortable setup.
· Position the ball off your left heel.
· Position your head over the golf ball.
· Set your hands slightly forward.
· Stroke the ball on the upswing.
· Keep the putter low.
· Establish a good tempo.
· Work at practice.

Lasting Impressions

One common fault of most amateur golfers is that they "talk themselves out of putts" by overreading the greens. All too often these players study the line of their putt first from behind the ball, then from the right side of the line, then the opposite side of the ball, and finally from the left side of the line. Why do they do this? They just happened to see some hotshot do it on television the week before. Trouble is, that big-name pro probably missed the putt after reading it from four different angles. Indeed, as you read a putt, try to let your first impression be your last impression. In other words, if you stand behind the ball and notice that it will break from left to right, sell yourself on the fact that it will break that way. Checking the line from other angles will only create indecision. Besides, reading greens from several angles wastes considerable time, and slows play for everyone.

Routine Putting

If you take the time to study the actions of golf's best players as they prepare to putt the ball, you will notice that they always repeat a set pattern of movements before they strike it. In golf, as in all sports, it is important that the player establish a groove, a definite movement pattern, in order to approach the ball in a precise and relaxed way every time.

Some suggestions:

1. Stand alongside your ball, assume your normal putting stance, and then take one or two short practice strokes. After that, wipe the face of the putter

against the inside of one of your pant legs or against your shoe to remove anything that might affect the roll of the ball, take a deep breath—and make your putt.

2. Stand well behind the ball on a line approximating the line of the putt and then take a practice stroke or two, all the while imagining what will happen to the ball once it leaves the face of the putter. In other words, try to see the putt even before you hit it. After that, wipe the face of the putter, step forward, take a deep breath—and make the putt.

3. Walk to a point about halfway between your ball and the cup, look both ways—at the ball and at the cup—and then take a practice stroke or two along a line that approximates the line of your putt. By doing this, you will acquire a feel for what the putt will do—that is, how it will roll—over the last half of its trip to the cup. Then move to the ball, wipe off the face of the putter, take a deep breath—and make the putt.

Spot Putting

On long putts it usually is difficult, if not impossible, to keep the line and the target within your peripheral vision as you address the ball. As a result, many golfers tend to putt blindly when they cannot see the entire line. One way to curb this blindness is to "spot" putt, something good putters do automatically. As you line up a long putt, simply pick out a certain spot over which the ball must roll during the first 5 to 10 feet and then use that spot as your first target. This spot can be a strand of grass with a different shade, an old ball mark or spike mark, or even an old cup. Anything will do. By spot putting, you will get your ball rolling along the intended line immediately.

Stroke Saving

Unfortunately, not all tee shots come to rest exactly 250 yards down the middle of the fairway, not all approach shots stop at the lip of the cup, and not all putts drop into the hole. Indeed, for every pure striker of the ball who walks down the fairway and struts around the green, there are hundreds of scramblers who spend their time extricating themselves from the various hazards spread throughout a golf course. For these scramblers—and their number includes many top-level touring professionals—the name of the game is "stroke saving."

As the scramblers like to say, there is no room on the scorecard for explanations. By that, they mean that a par four is a par four regardless of how you make it. A 250-yard drive down the middle, a seven-iron approach to fifteen feet, then two easy putts—a routine par four. And a 210-yard drive snap hooked into the left gully, a nine-iron blast back onto the fairway, a delicate approach to 8 feet, then a solid putt into the back of the cup—well, that's hardly routine but it's still a four. No explanations needed, thank you.

There are all types of scrambling shots. A sand shot is a scrambling shot, because you are not supposed to be in the sand in the first place. A

121

On recovery shots from bunkers, the objective is to keep the face of your sand wedge open, pop the ball into the air, and make it land softly, as Jack Nicklaus does here.

shot from a downhill-sidehill lie qualifies as a scrambling shot, because you must make a number of alterations in your setup and your swing in order to hit the ball properly. A pitch-and-run shot from 30 yards is a scrambling shot for the most part, because you probably would not be 30 yards short of the green unless you had missed one or more shots en route.

In playing many of these so-called scrambling shots, it is important that you always think ahead. As you deliberate over a shot, always make a firm decision as to where you want the ball to end up. Don't approach a scrambling shot thinking, "Well, maybe the ball will clear the tree and get into the fairway." Instead, play the shot that will get the ball where you want it—the safest place you can logically expect to reach—without fail. The trick is to do the best you can with what you have. As a result, the best scrambling shot usually is the one that leaves you with a good clear shot at the pin with your *next* swing.

For example, let's imagine that you have hit your tee shot into a gully on the left side of the fairway, approximately 210 yards off the tee and some 150 yards from the center of the green. As you survey the shot from the gully, you notice that the grass is fairly thick and slightly wet and that you will have to assume a stance in which your feet will be slightly above the ball. Also, the wall of the gully is relatively close to your ball, and there are several weeping willow trees down the left side of the rough between your ball and the green. There are two ways to approach the execution of this shot:

1. You can attempt to play a miracle recovery shot by opening the face of your five- or six-iron, chopping powerfully down on the ball, and then praying that the ball will clear the wall of the gully, avoid the weeping willows, and carry onto the green. The chance of such a result is perhaps less than one in a hundred; the chances that the ball will stay in the gully, drop among the weeping willows, or find some other hazard are perhaps ninety in a hundred.

2. You can attempt to play a safe recovery shot by taking out your pitching wedge or your nine-iron, spotting a location in the fairway that offers a straight-in shot to the pin, and then hitting a safe recovery to that preferred area.

That second option is, of course, the right thing to do. It offers not only a safe extrication from the gully but also the best possible third shot to the green. Remember this: Once you are in trouble on the golf course, the first thing you want to do is to get out of that trouble. Don't flirt with more danger.

This chapter explains how to play the scrambling shots you will encounter most frequently during a round of golf. Shots such as the backhanded swipe with the back side of a five-iron, attempted while you hang from a tree, are omitted from the discussion, since such shots require invention, not technique.

SAND SHOTS

The best way to handle sand traps is to stay out of them. But avoiding bunkers is about as easy as avoiding income taxes. Municipal golf courses generally try to keep bunkers to a minimum, mainly for reasons of maintenance expense, but even they have an average of at least one per hole. Private golf courses, however, often look more like sandy beaches than anything else; many of the best private layouts have between a hundred and two hundred bunkers on them, and one famed course, the Pine Valley Golf Club in Clementon, New Jersey, probably has five times more sand than grass on its property. As a sand-weary player once said of Pine Valley, "This place was made for camels."

One thing the visitor to Pine Valley and other sand-infested layouts learns fast is that there is no such thing as the basic sand shot. However, bunker shots do fall into broad categories, with a different recovery swing necessary for each. Here are the types of sand shots you will most likely be forced to play during a normal round of golf—and the respective ways to extricate your ball from the sand. A "normal round" assumes that your luck is not so bad that you are faced with a one leg in, one leg out, uphill, embedded, against-the-lip sand shot each time you play. Such shots require a "hit and pray" technique and practically defy logical instruction.

The Green-side Explosion

This comes closest to being the basic sand shot. Here the ball has landed in, or rolled into, a bunker alongside the green, but it is sitting pretty—meaning that it is not deeply embedded in the sand. Still, the bunker is below the level of the putting surface, and the ball must pop into the air, clear the lip of the bunker, land on the green, and then pull up short—within what you hope is easy putting distance of the cup.

In playing this shot, which is called an explosion because the ball must explode from the sand and thus spray loose bits of sand in its path, the trick is to keep the face of your sand wedge open throughout the entire swing. If you don't, the club head will burrow into the sand and turn in, and as a result the ball either will fail to leave the sand or will fly line-drive style across the green and into even more trouble. To keep the club face open, make certain that your right hand never passes over or even across the left hand at impact; to put it another way, always keep your right hand under your left hand.

The stance for the explosion shot must be open, with the left foot set on a path that runs against the instep of the right foot, not on a line parallel to

The green-side sand shot. Dig your feet into the sand until the spikes take a good hold; you cannot afford any slippage while in a bunker. Your feet are now slightly below the level of the ball in the sand, so shorten up on the club

just a bit. At address, set up so the ball is off your left heel and your hands
are well forward, opposite your left leg. The length of the backswing is
governed in part by the distance between your ball and the target.

Strike the club into the sand approximately one full ball behind your ball, and don't baby the swing. As you hit the ball, keep your right hand under your left and continue to a high finish. Don't quit on a bunker shot or you will probably get the chance to try another explosion shot with your next swing.

the target line. And, so that you're balanced and firmly set, dig your feet into the sand until the spikes take a good hold, and adopt a stance that is just a bit wider than your normal one. The worst thing that can happen during a sand trap shot is the loss of footing; once this happens, you lose all control.

As you settle into the sand, both feet will end up slightly below the level of the ball. To compensate, shorten up on the grip of the club by about one inch. Now, as you address the ball, set yourself in a position where the ball rests a few inches off your left heel, as it does for normal golf shots.

At address, your hands must be positioned well ahead of the ball, at a point that is on a direct line with your left leg. If the hands are set on a line that is either even with or behind the ball, you will be forced to lift the club sharply on the backswing in order to keep it from grounding against the hazard; then on the downswing you will necessarily strike the sand prematurely and make contact with the ball on too flat a plane, producing a "skulled" line-drive shot in some errant direction. (According to the rules of golf, you cannot ground the club head against the sand until you are at the point of impact; in fact, it is an automatic one-stroke penalty if you do ground your club in any hazard prior to the actual hitting of the ball.)

Now you are ready to execute the explosion. As a general rule, both the distance between your ball and the pin and the texture of the sand will determine how sharply and how deeply you blast with your club. The shorter the shot, the deeper you dig into the sand; the longer the shot, the shallower you dig into the sand—or, to put it another way, the more you skim the ball. On all explosion-type bunker shots, though, you should strike into the sand approximately one full ball behind your ball's position. By doing this, you allow the big flange of the sand wedge to cut smoothly through the sand and pop the ball out of the bunker, not line-drive it out. You should use about double the swing force you would apply to a regular pitch shot from a similar distance; in other words, if the bunker shot must travel a distance of 15 yards, swing with about the force you would apply to a 30-yard pitch shot. And execute a high follow-through.

Remember: As you swing the club through the explosion shot, always keep the right hand under the left; if you don't, you will close the club face and consequently drill the ball, not explode it. And once you have blasted the ball from the bunker, remember to take a rake and smooth out the foot and club prints that you made in the sand.

On the fried-egg bunker shot, keep 75 percent of your body weight on your left side, close the club face, and aim for the mound behind your buried ball.

The Fried Egg

On courses where the sand is very soft and very fine—or very wet—high approach shots that fall into bunkers usually plug deeply into their landing spot. Indeed, there is no harder bunker shot to play than the buried lie, where some part—or even all—of the ball is embedded in sand, making it look like a fried egg. From such lies, it is almost impossible to execute a recovery shot that will get the ball close to the hole; the best shot from a fried-egg lie is any shot that removes the ball from the bunker.

In setting up to play the ball from a fried-egg lie, close the face of the club, turning it inward, then position the ball in the middle of your open stance, and place perhaps 75 percent of your body weight on your left side. Once again, the distance between your ball and the pin determines how sharply and how deeply you blast into the sand with your club. Now the ball is surrounded by a circular mound of sand—the fried-egg effect. Play the shot by trying to knock down the back mound—which may be a ball's width in back of your ball. After impact, keep the club working with good firmness so that it can cut under the ball and pop it into the air. Remember, you must keep your right hand under your left throughout the swing; the club head is closed at impact, and if you then turn the right hand over the left, the ball will either go nowhere or fly uncontrollably across the green.

Hard or Wet Sand

Explosion shots from hard or wet sand rarely prove effective, mainly because the flange of a sand wedge will bounce off, rather than cut smoothly under, this kind of sand. And when a sand wedge bounces, the ball invariably takes a line-drive trajectory and does not return to earth until it is well past its intended landing area. As a result, the best way to approach hard or wet sand shots is to use a pitching wedge, not a sand wedge, and try to skim the ball out of the bunker, not explode it.

To skim the ball, take a slightly narrower stance than normal, set yourself firmly in the sand, shorten up on the club by about an inch, and then take a swing that is quite restricted in terms of body movement. The more you move during a skim shot, the greater the chance that you will lose control of the club and bury it into the sand. In skimming, keep your hands well ahead of the ball and aim at a target half a ball behind the position of your ball as it rests in the sand. Take some sand at impact, but don't dig the club too deeply—or the ball will go nowhere. The follow-through should approximate the length of the backswing; the length of both, of course, depends on the distance the ball must travel to reach its intended target.

Fairway Traps

Since the early 1950s, most golf architects have designed courses with fairway bunkering that in no way resembles the fairway bunkering seen on those great

Have no fear; hitting a wood shot from a fairway bunker is very practical. Set your feet firmly, don't ground the club, and take a swing that is somewhat more restricted than your normal swing with a fairway wood. The trick is to hit the ball before you make contact with the sand.

old courses created by Mother Nature and such legendary architects as Tillinghast, Ross, and Mackenzie. In the old days a fairway bunker—basically, any trap that is either in the fairway or alongside it, presenting a shot that requires something more than a sand-wedge explosion for the player to reach the green —was employed as a penalty; if you hit the ball into one of the pot bunkers at, say, St. Andrews, or into an aperture at Pine Valley, you might well have to play your extrication(s) back in the direction of the tee.

Nowadays, though, most fairway bunkers tend to be natural extensions of the fairway or the rough; in essence, sand has been substituted for the grass.

Modern fairway bunkers rarely feature high lips or deep bottoms. The only real problem they present is psychological: "Oh, no, I'm in another trap."

Actually, the fairway bunker shot is by far the easiest of all sand shots to play, provided that the ball has not plugged deeply into the sand. As you survey the shot, look first at the lip over which the ball must travel in order to fly out of the trap. Then select a club that will comfortably provide enough instant height so that your ball will clear the lip, however high it might be, with ease. Never gamble in the matter of club selection when playing from a fairway bunker. If you think your four-iron offers only a 75–25 chance of getting a ball over the lip and out of the trap, play a five-iron instead.

In setting up over the ball, assume a normal stance, digging your feet into the sand until they take a firm hold. Choke up on the club about one inch, and put 75 percent of your weight on your front foot. You do not want to hit behind the ball when playing from a fairway bunker, as you do in most other sand shots. Instead, you want to hit the ball *first*—and then the sand. As such, you should aim at a point in the sand that is approximately one ball *in front of* your ball as it rests in the bunker. Then just make a normal swing with a solid follow-through.

One suggestion: If the lip of the bunker presents no problem with club selection, always take one club *more*—a five-iron, say, rather than a six—than you would use for a shot of similar length from the fairway. Also, if there is no lip to contend with, don't be afraid to play a wood from a fairway bunker. On the whole, fairway bunkers really are just sandy fairways.

The Texas Wedge

In case you are not from the Lone Star State, or have never played golf with a Texan, the Texas wedge is a simple old putter. Actually, it is any putter that is used when a player decides to putt a ball out of a sand trap, when a putt is the safest and surest way to get a ball onto the green. In order to play a Texas wedge shot, though, the ball must be perched atop the sand, not plugged into it. Also, the area between the ball and the pin must be relatively flat and level. You cannot play a Texas wedge if there is a lip between your ball and the pin, or if there is a wide expanse of thick, bushy grass between the edge of the bunker and the edge of the green; a lip will stop the roll of the ball, and bushy grass will deaden its roll.

To play the Texas wedge, assume your normal putting stance and use your normal putting stroke. Then hit the ball more on the toe of the blade in order to get it rolling immediately. The rest is a matter of touch and feel.

The 40- to 60-Yard Wedge Shot

If you can execute the 40- to 60-yard wedge shot with some degree of proficiency, accuracy, feel, and finesse, you can save at least four shots a round. The trick is to hit the ball close enough to the hole so that you will have a reasonable chance of making the putt for your birdie, par, bogey, or whatever. Getting the ball up and down in two strokes from 40 to 60 yards away is what distinguishes the good players from the bad, the winners from the losers.

The trouble is, most golfers don't *hit* this shot. Instead, they flip the ball toward the target with a long, loose swing. However, the longer and leaner the swing, the less direction, feel, touch, and finesse there will be to the shot. The right club for this shot is the pitching wedge, not the sand wedge, which has a big flange and tends to bounce off the turf; the pitching wedge is easier to control.

In setting up, take a stance that is slightly narrower than normal and open it slightly by moving your left foot back a few inches. At address, the ball should be in the middle of your stance, and most of your body weight on your left side. Only a minimum amount of body movement, please, during this shot. One sure way to restrict movement—to prevent body sway—is to push your right knee in a bit and plant the inside of your right foot squarely into the turf. When Gary Player executes this shot, the inside of his right foot is planted so firmly in the ground that the outside of his right foot is actually in the air. By establishing such a rigid position for the right side, Player develops a solid base to work from.

Instead of a long, loose swing, take a short, compact swing with plenty of force and feel. Make solid contact with the ball. As you hit it, make certain that you do not collapse your left elbow. Keep your hands firm, never allowing them to get too loose or wristy, and strike the ball while the face of the club is reaching the end of its downward arc. Then, after impact, swing the club through the ball, taking a healthy divot, and into its follow-through, keeping the club head on line to the target. Don't break down at the left wrist.

Constant practice is the best way to learn this stroke-saving shot. You should practice with your pitching wedge at least as often as you practice with your driver and your putter; the driver, the putter, and the pitching wedge are the three clubs that you normally employ most often during a round of golf. When you work on this shot, always practice to a target; otherwise you will not acquire the necessary touch and feel for it. A target can be anything: a towel placed on a practice range, a bush, a tree, a sand trap, a green.

A   B

c

The stroke saver. Getting the ball into the hole in two strokes from 25 to 50 yards is one sure way to happier golf. Take a slightly narrower, slightly open stance (A and B), with the ball back toward the right foot, and then turn your right knee in just a bit to restrict unwanted body movement. The swing should be short (C), firm, and compact, leading to a solid striking of the ball. Don't lazy the club into this shot; control it with a firm hit. After impact, make a natural follow-through.

A   B

THE CUT SHOT

One of the prettiest shots in golf is the cut shot, a short-iron approach—hit with anything from, say, a seven-iron to a sand wedge—which, heavy with backspin, lands on a green, takes one bounce, and either stops dead or begins to roll tantalizingly back to a position near where it first landed. When played as planned, it is the ultimate control shot. Most pros play the cut shot so well that, as the saying goes, they seem to be able to make the ball dance. But it is such a finesse shot that you must practice it constantly if you expect to be consistently effective with it.

C

The cut shot. Hit correctly, the ball will land on the green, take one bounce, and either stop dead or roll back a few feet. To hit this shot, take an open stance (A), setting up with your left foot away from the target, then take the club back well to the outside and swing on an outside-inside plane (B). In these illustrations, the club head follows the long, straight line, while the ball takes off in the direction of the angled line (C).

To put backspin on a ball, you must first have a good lie to work with. In setting up, assume your normal stance, but play the ball slightly back of center. The most important aspect of the cut shot is that you must keep your hands well ahead of the ball at address. By doing this, the hands will lead the club head through the ball, enabling the club head to strike the ball *before* it strikes the turf, thereby creating the desired backspin effect. If the club strikes the turf before it reaches the ball, grass will come between club head and ball at impact and kill the desired backspin. Therefore, your impact target should be about the middle of the golf ball. At impact, you must hit hard with your right hand, but at the same time you must not allow the right hand to over-power the left. After impact, continue to a normal high follow-through finish.

HARD-PAN SHOTS

Hard pan is a golfing euphemism for turf that is hard and skimmed down, and also for bare ground. To play a decent shot on this kind of surface, the trick is to pick the ball off it as cleanly as possible, hitting the ball before the club head makes contact with the hard surface and bounces in some erratic fashion. Set up with the ball slightly back in your stance, making certain that your hands are well ahead of the ball at address. If the hands are too far back, they will ultimately cause the club head to hit the ground before the ball—the one thing you don't want to happen. Hit properly, a shot from hard pan will take a lower flight than normal and, after landing, will probably run a considerable distance.

GRASS SHOTS

Wet Grass

Controlling a golf ball from a wet-grass lie is a tricky proposition because the ball tends to shoot out of such lies without very much spin and to fly somewhat higher than normal. In many ways, a wet-grass ball looks much like a knuckleball, because water comes between the blade of the club head and the ball, thus eliminating any consistent spin. So, use one club less—a six-iron, say, rather than a five—than you normally would for a shot from a similar distance.

Thick, Bushy Grass

When you hit the ball into thick, bushy grass around the green, realize that you have made a mistake and that, barring a miracle recovery, you will have to pay the price for your blunder. As you inspect a ball settled in heavy grass, don't dream up some high-risk shot, because it usually will lead to some very high numbers on your scorecard. Once you are in the thick stuff, be happy to settle for an extrication that will leave you within two-putt range.

The right club to use in these situations is the sand wedge, which will provide maximum lift and height. In setting up, assume a slightly open stance and play the ball off the left heel. Open the face of the club at address. The swing for this shot must be more upright than the swing for a regular sand-wedge shot, and you must make certain that you hit the ball hard enough to dislodge

On delicate stroke-saving shots from around the green, shorten up on the club for better control and accuracy.

it from the grass and get it onto the green. Don't baby this shot, or else you may have it for your next shot, as well.

Fringe play. Stroke this chip shot from the fringe much as you stroke a putt. Shorten up on the grip, play the ball back toward your right foot, land the ball on the green, and then let it roll to the hole. The swing should be short and firm.

PLAYING FROM THE FRINGE

Your ball has stopped on the fringe or collar of the green and is, say, 5 feet from the putting surface. Do you chip the ball with an iron—a combination shot in which the ball is sent airborne for a brief moment before rolling to the target —or putt it? It all depends.

If the total distance between your ball and the pin is less than, say, 30 feet, you definitely should putt the ball. Your worst putt will probably be as good as your best chip. It is much easier to control the roll of a putt from such a relatively close distance than it is to control the flight and roll of a chip shot from a similar distance.

However, if the total distance between your ball and the pin is more than 30 feet, you should play a chip shot—unless the contour of the green dictates otherwise. For instance, it is usually wiser to putt, not chip, when you are faced with a downhill shot from the fringe.

The advantage of the chip shot is that you don't have to negotiate a roll over the long-grass collar of the green. Most skilled amateurs approach a chip shot with the same confidence that they approach a putt. Most high-handicap amateurs, however, seem terrified when confronted by a chip shot, and as a result they usually—and wisely—opt for the safety of their putter.

THE CHIP SHOT

In most ways, the chip shot from 10 yards or less off the green should be regarded as another form of putt. The chip shot can well be the greatest stroke saver in the high handicapper's arsenal. For one thing, high handicappers invariably must play more chip shots than low handicappers; high handicappers, of course, do not hit their long- or mid- or even short-iron approach shots onto the putting surface with the regularity that low handicappers do.

In chipping, the trick is to have the ball roll, not fly, as much as possible. It is far easier to control a rolling golf ball than it is to control an airborne golf ball. So keep it low. To play the chip shot successfully, you must have a good sense of feel and touch for the particular shot. You should chip with a five-iron or a six-iron, or perhaps even a seven-iron if the distance between your ball and the cup is fairly short. Many older golfers use a specially made "chipper" for these shots; this club looks much like a putter, but it has a longer shaft and some 25 degrees of loft built into the face of the club, which usually is approximately the size of a blade putter.

To chip, set up in a stance that resembles your putting stance. Be certain to set your hands in front of the ball too, because you want to chip the ball while the club head is still on its descent. The backswing should be short and firm, and the hit itself must be firm and precise. It is important that your wrists break only minimally, if at all, during this chipping process; breaking the wrists on such a short, delicate shot often leads to the dreaded chili dip—a fluffed shot that travels about three feet.

Chip shots are easy to practice, too. For one thing, you don't have to go to the practice range and rent a bucket of balls in order to practice chip shots; you can simply take a handful of your own golf balls, or your practice shag balls, and chip them to a pin position on the practice putting green. For another, you don't have to get outfitted in your golfing garb to practice chip shots; many a prominent player stops by his local club and, still wearing his shirt and tie, works on his chipping for 45 minutes or so a few nights a week.

By practicing the chip shot, you will acquire a familiarity with the various clubs—five-, six-, and/or seven-iron—used most often in chipping situations. Better still, you will acquire a feel for the most important aspects of the chipping game: How long the ball should be in the air, and how long it should be rolling. There is no standard answer for this question, mainly because there really is no such thing as the standard golf shot. But by practicing your chip shots, you will definitely gain a feeling for the shot and how to play it.

HILLY LIES

Perhaps the only way to avoid having to face a so-called "hilly lie" during a round of golf is to move to the Texas Panhandle. Hilly lies are more often the rule than the exception on the great majority of golf courses throughout the world, particularly the older-style courses built before the golf boom of the late 1950s. Courses such as Merion, Oakmont, Augusta National, Olympic, Medinah, and Oakland Hills were designed in such a way that the golfer might not encounter a perfectly flat lie at any point during the round. That's the rub of the green, as they say.

Before discussing the four basic types of hilly lies, a few words of advice. There is one way to avoid a particularly tricky hilly lie: Don't hit your ball there. For instance, as an amateur golfer, you no doubt play the same course

nine rounds out of ten, so you know where the difficult hilly lies are on that
course. Let's take an imaginary hole: a 375-yard par four that goes straight out
from the tee for the first 230 yards and then takes a deep downward dip for
75 yards before leveling off in front of the green. There are two ways to play
this hole:

1. You can try to hit a prodigious drive, one that will carry the 230 yards
of the level fairway, land on the downside of the hill, and then roll all the way
to the bottom of the hill, stopping on a level lie.

2. Or you can take out a three-wood, a four-wood, or even a one- or
two-iron and lay up short of the downslope, leaving yourself with, say, a
150-yard approach into the green from a lie that is relatively level.

What should you do? Take the safe way out, of course, and hit a safe tee
shot that stops short of the hill. There is no reason whatsoever to risk the
prodigious tee shot that might, but most likely will not, carry to the bottom of
the hill. Also, what happens to golfers when they try to overswing and over-
power the ball? They mis-hit it. On the whole, a 150-yard approach from a level
lie is a far easier shot to maneuver than a 100-yard approach from a severe
downhill lie.

The Downhill Lie

As you address a downhill lie, place the majority of your weight on your front
foot and keep all body movement to a minimum. Also, in playing the downhill
lie you should stand in a position that is slightly more upright than normal; by
doing this, you will better control the path of the moving club head. At address,
too, the ball should be back in your stance, at least at a point where it is halfway
between your feet. The reason for this is that the prevailing lie dictates that the
club will hit the ball earlier than usual at a point between your right foot and
the middle of the stance. In playing the downhill lie, you should pick the club
up a bit on the takeaway to keep it from stubbing against the grass and thus
turning in your hands. Also, downhill shots will fly lower and travel a greater
distance than shots of a similar distance from level lies; so, take one club less,
a five-iron, say, instead of a four, when you're hitting the ball from a downhill
lie. The position of your shoulders at address ought to follow, roughly, the
contour of the land, meaning they should be parallel to the ground. And
remember: Don't quit on the swing after making impact.

On a downhill lie, shorten up on the grip, play the ball well back in your stance, and put your weight forward. Don't overswing.

With an uphill lie, play the ball forward in your stance, and don't fall back.

The Uphill Lie

The uphill lie is a much easier situation to handle than the downhill lie. The real trick is not to fall off the shot; you can't allow your body weight to collapse onto your right side during this swing. If that happens, you will snap a hook. So restrict your body movement, never letting your body weight pass the inside of your right foot. There is no need to alter the standard position of the ball at address; keep it off your right foot. As in the downhill lie, you should stand in a slightly more upright position than normal, with your shoulders parallel to the ground. Unlike the downhill lie, this shot will travel *higher* and travel a *shorter* distance than a shot of a similar distance from a level lie. As such, just take one *more* club than you normally would, a four-iron, say, instead of a five, when you're hitting the ball from an uphill lie. Also, don't fight the hill; let your swing work with the hill, not against it.

For a downhill-sidehill lie, plant your feet, imagine you are sitting in a chair, and swing in a very restricted manner, aiming slightly left of your target.

The Downhill-Sidehill Lie

Playing a shot when the ball is below your feet is extremely difficult and often comical; players tend to contort themselves like pretzels as they try to find a comfortable stance over the ball. The simplest way to address this type of shot is to "sit down" into the ball. Think of it this way. As you address the downhill-sidehill lie, imagine that you are sitting down on a chair. By doing this, you will set your weight properly on your heels. Now the trick is to restrict your body movement almost totally; any extra body movement will throw you completely off balance and produce a forgettable shot. As you set up for the downhill-sidehill lie, your target should be a point well left of your intended landing position; the contour of the hill will automatically produce a left-to-right movement of the ball. Allow for this. Then swing within yourself, playing a controlled type of shot, hit mostly with the arms and hands.

When faced with an uphill-sidehill lie, shorten up on the grip, lean into the shot, and aim slightly to the right.

The Uphill-Sidehill Lie

This is a considerably easier shot to play than the downhill-sidehill lie. Here your body weight should be moved forward, almost totally onto your toes; under no circumstances do you want to fall back on this shot and have your weight on your heels. Also, you should address the ball in a more upright manner and choke down on the grip of the club. Again, you want to restrict your body movement, letting the hands and the arms do the majority of the work in the swing. The natural tendency with a shot from an uphill-sidehill lie is to hook the ball or pull it. To compensate for this, aim slightly to the right of your target.

7

Last Words

Golf is a sport, a game to be played for enjoyment. As an amateur, you do not play golf for a living, so let the game be what it should: a pleasant retreat from the week-long madness and drudgery of the rest of your life. Don't let golf become bigger than it is, or you will have destroyed the purpose —and the beauty—of the game.

Golf works best when the player uses the game as a salve, not as a cause. At the same time, you should not just walk onto the golf course, yell "Fore!" and play away. There are definite ways to prepare yourself for a round of golf, mentally as well as physically.

In thinking about your swing and about the shots you want to hit, try to use what golf pros call positive thoughts. The best way to do this is to avoid using "don't" as part of your golfing vocabulary. As you stand over a shot, tell yourself, "Take the club back smoothly now," rather than, "Don't take the club back too quickly, dummy." Use positive psychology, not negative psychology.

One way to improve your scores is to know your golf course. Most amateur golfers play the same course all the time, but they probably do not know much more about their layout than its name. Indeed, if you play the same course with

149

Pat Bradley celebrates a putt that dropped into the cup for a birdie.

any frequency, you should always carry an annotated scorecard with you that details the exact yardages to the green from various spots on each hole. Knowing your golf course may well save you three or four shots a round.

Pacing off a golf course is a simple matter. Go out onto the fairway and pick out a spot where your average drive usually lands. Now look for a permanent marker in the immediate vicinity of that spot—say, a tree or a rock or a sand trap alongside, or a sprinkler head in the middle of, the fairway. Then pace off the yardages from your marker to the front of the green, the middle of the green, and the back of the green. Take a scorecard and note the distances to each point on the green from that marking point. Let's say that from the marker the distance to the fifth hole at your club is 110 yards to the front of the green, 124 yards to the middle, and 138 yards to the back.

All right, suppose, the next time you play the fifth hole, you miss your tee shot a bit and the ball stops well short of your normal landing area. To calculate the distance from that spot to the pin, simply pace the yardage from your ball to your marking point—let's say that it is 22 yards—and then check out the location of the pin, which this day happens to be at the back of the green, or some 138 yards from your marker. Add 138 and 22, and you have a 160-yard shot to the pin. By knowing this yardage, you eliminate guesswork from the matter of club selection. For you, 160 yards may mean a five-iron—and now you can hit that five-iron with confidence, knowing that it is the right club for the shot.

Similarly, you should establish distance parameters with each club in your bag—and then let these parameters dictate your club selection. For instance, to determine the range for, say, your five-iron, hit about a half dozen five-iron shots and then pace off the yardage each ball traveled. The mean average of those five-iron shots will provide an excellent indicator of exactly how far you normally hit your five-iron, while the respective distances covered by each ball will provide some very definite parameters regarding your five-iron. Knowing the mean average and the parameters of a club also helps eliminate any indecision about club selection as you stand on the fairway and look at the green. If the pin is 165 yards from your ball, and you hit your five-iron between 160 and 170 yards, the five-iron is the right club for the shot. Not an easy four-iron or a hard six-iron, just a normal five-iron.

Write your potential with each club on the same scorecard as your distance figures. It will make your golf more enjoyable—and more rewarding.

Another way to improve your game is to keep tabs on yourself. Unfortunately, most golfers play a round of golf, post their score, and then forget about their game until they show up on the first tee for their next round. However,

The Apawamis Club

	MEN				HOLE #	WOMEN			DEPTH GREEN
	BLUE	WHITE	HDCP	PAR	(note)	PAR	HDCP	RED	↓
HILTON'S ROCK	356	356	10	4	155 / Tree LEFT	4	5	351	62'
HILLSIDE	390	381	6	4	150 / 3rd Tree Left	4	5	305	64' / 52'
THE DIPPER	315	312	16	4	80 / Sprinkler head top of hill	4	15	265	44'
THE PLATEAU	324	302	12	4	73 / From end of cartpath	4	7	294	71'
THE DELL	149	138	18	3	152 / Stanton	3	17	131	79'
SUNNYSIDE	319	300	14	4	66 / End of bunker-right	4	11	291	44'
THE GORGE	409	401	2	4	186 / Willow on right	4	1	383	56'
WOODSIDE	362	343	8	4	143 / Willow on right	4	9	320	49'
BROADWAY	582	551	4	5	136 / Lone tree on right	5	3	493	64'
OUT	3206	3084		36		36		2833	
LAND ENDS	513	493	7	5	92 / End of water left	5	4	472	53'
THE BRIDGE	358	343	5	4	122 / Sprinkler head top of hill	4	8	307	49'
BUNKER HILL	203	171	15	3	222 / Back of tree	4	14	156	54'
THE POND	346	324	11	4	114 / First willow left	4	10	296	51'
WATER LOO	446	381	3	4	226 / Rock on right	4	6	446	58'
TRIBULATION	412	401	1	4	184 / Last pine right	4	2	398	52'
CONSOLATION	180	177	13	3	191 / Back of tree	3	16	150	61'
SLEEPY HOLLOW	501	491	9	5	83 / S-head top of hill	5	12	456	66'
HOME	321	297	17	4	77 / First bush on left	4	18	285	62'
IN	3280	3078		36		37		2966	
TOTAL	6486	6162		72		73		5799	

MGA RATING 70.7	MGA RATING 69.1	HANDICAP				WMGA RATING 72.3
		NET SCORE				

DATE — SIGNED: — ATTESTED: — MATCH +

The smart golfer's secret weapon: an annotated scorecard.

if you want to improve your golf, if you want to be serious about the game, maintain a set of very simple charts that detail your round-by-round performance. By keeping these records, you also will be able to detect any deterioration in certain parts of your game—and make corrections before it is too late. Some golfers keep elaborate charts filled with graphs and multicolored lines, but such effort is not necessary. In fact, all the information you need to keep tabs on your game can be kept in a little notebook or on a single large sheet of paper.

As you review your round-by-round performances and compare them with previous rounds, you will be able to detect those areas of the game that are in good repair and those that need help. For instance, you may well discover from reading your charts that you are missing seven or eight fairways to the left side in each round. Knowing this, you can head to the practice tee and work out the problem—whatever it might be—that is causing those dead-left tee shots.

Finally, golfers, like all other athletes, must maintain a certain fitness level if they expect to be able to perform well at their game. Between rounds, you can keep your wrists and hands strong by squeezing a rubber ball or a wrist-exercising device for five or ten minutes a day. You can do this almost any place or any time—in your car, at the office, or perhaps while watching television at night. Legs are a vital part of the golf swing, and one way to keep your legs in shape is to jog in place for a couple of minutes each day—or, better yet, to jog around the neighborhood for a mile or two. If your legs are not in good condition, you will not only get very tired as you play the last few holes of your round, but you will lose some of the power generated by your legs during the swing.

Also, before you play a round of golf, you should limber up for about five minutes by doing various stretching exercises.

And no golfer should ever play a round of golf unless he or she has hit at least a dozen practice shots. Start with a couple of loose and easy swings with a short iron, move to a middle iron, then a long iron, and, finally, hit four or five tee shots. Then go to the putting green and stroke some putts. Start with a couple of 25- or 30-footers and finish with a couple of 3- or 4-footers. Always hole your last practice putt, too. It's an old golfing superstition that makes sense.

The saying is that practice makes perfect. While there is no such creature as a perfect golfer, practice will indeed take some of the kinks out of your game, make you a better shot maker, and thus make you a happier individual.

Now play away and have fun. And remember: Do it your way. As you will discover, on the golf course, *your* way is the better way.

Golf Etiquette

Golf is a civilized sport. When you are on the course, please show respect for the course and also for your playing partner(s) and your opponent(s).

—*Never* move when another player is in the act of hitting a shot.

—*Never* talk when another player is in the act of hitting a shot.

—*Never* stand in another player's line when that player is in the act of hitting a shot.

—*Never* hit your shot until all the golfers playing ahead of you are well out of range.

—*Never* slow up a course by keeping the players behind you waiting while you search for a lost ball.

—*Never* dillydally on the course.

—*Never* leave footprints in a bunker. Smooth them out with a rake or your club *after*—never before—hitting your shot.

—*Always* replace divots after hitting your shot.

—*Always* repair ball marks made on the green, something that can be done easily with a tee or with a pronged implement available in all pro shops.

—*Never* display anger by throwing your golf club in disgust.

Glossary

Bent. A finely textured species of grass used for putting greens.

Bermuda. A coarsely textured species of grass in which the strands intertwine used for both fairways and putting greens, especially in hot, humid climates.

Birdie. A hole scored in one stroke less than par.

Bogey. In America, a hole played in one stroke more than par. In Great Britain, the number of strokes a better-than-average player is expected to take for a hole.

Dog leg. A hole whose fairway is marked by an acute bend.

Draw. A slight hook in the flight of a ball.

Eagle. A hole played in two strokes less than par on a par-four or par-five.

Fade. To hit the ball with a left-to-right spin.

Fore! A cry of warning to other players or to spectators.

Four-ball match. One in which two play their better ball against the better ball of two other players.

Halve. A hole is said to be halved if each side holes out in the same number of strokes.

Handicap. The number of strokes over par in which one's average game is played. This number may be deducted from that player's actual score in medal play-net competition.

Hazard. An area, such as a bunker or a pond, in which the privileges of play are restricted.

Honor. The privilege of playing first from a tee, which cannot be declined.

Hook. To hit the ball with a right-to-left spin.

Hosel. The socket into which the shaft of an iron is fitted.

155

Links.   Originally, a course laid out on linksland, the sandy soil deposited by centuries of receding oceanic tides. Today, unfortunately, it has become a synonym for any golf course.

Match play.   A tournament or championship conducted under the rules of match rather than those of stroke play.

Medal.   The low qualifying score for a match-play tournament or championship. Also, slang for a stroke-play competition.

Nassau.   Three matches in one. One point is allotted for the first nine holes, another point for the second nine, and still another for the overall eighteen.

Par.   The number of strokes an expert golfer is expected to make on each hole. It is determined by the length of the hole, although configuration and the severity of hazards has a bearing. A par-three is any hole up to 250 yards. A par-four is any hole between 251 and 470 yards. A par-five is any hole longer than 470. (For women these yardages run from 40 to 70 yards less.)

Pitch.   To lob, or loft, the ball into the air.

Pitch-and-run.   A shot so played that part of the desired distance is covered by the roll of the ball after it strikes the ground.

Pot bunker.   A small, deep sand trap.

Pull.   A wide, pronounced hook.

Push.   A shot that travels on a straight line but well to the right of the intended line.

Rough.   The part of the course that is not tee, fairway, green, or hazard.

Scratch player.   A player who has no handicap.

Shank.   The part of the hosel nearest the face. Also, to hit the ball on the shank.

Slice.   To hit the ball in such a way that it has a pronounced left-to-right spin, more so than a fade (the opposite of hook).